Harmony
and
Discord

Bishop Owen Dowling was a complex man whose long ministry sometimes attracted public controversy. This revealing and empathetic biography sheds considerable light on Owen's vision of God and vocation, worship and music, personal aspirations and human frailty. It offers a snapshot of Australian Anglicanism in the second half of the twentieth century and the challenges faced by its leaders.

Tom Frame
Director of St Mark's National Theological Centre, 2006-2014

I knew Owen in his retirement and endorse Bruce Stevens's frank – while generously appreciative – assessments. This little book is a labour of love both for Owen's memory and for a Church that is loved by God – as the presence of fine clergy like Owen shows – but which still has a lot to learn about the spiritual integration of sexuality.

Scott Cowdell
Canberra-based Anglican priest, theologian and writer

The life of
Bishop Owen Dowling
1934-2008

Harmony and Discord

Bruce Stevens

COVENTRY PRESS

Published in Australia by
Coventry Press
33 Scoresby Road
Bayswater VIC 3153

ISBN 9781922589347

Copyright © Bruce Stevens 2023

All rights reserved. Other than for the purposes and subject to the conditions prescribed under the *Copyright Act*, no part of this publication may be reproduced, stored in a retrieval system, or transmitted in any form or by any means, electronic, mechanical, photocopying, recording or otherwise, without the prior permission of the publisher.

Catalogue-in-Publication entry is available from the National Library of Australia
http://catalogue.nla.gov.au

Cover design by Ian James – www.jgd.com.au
Text design by Coventry Press
Set in EB Garamond

Printed in Australia

Contents

Foreword		6
Prelude		8
Chapter 1	A child	9
Chapter 2	University	18
Chapter 3	Life as a teacher	22
Chapter 4	Ordained for ministry	28
Chapter 5	The cathedral in Goulburn	33
Chapter 6	For a time ... in Wagga	39
Chapter 7	St John's, Canberra	45
Chapter 8	Life as an Assistant Bishop	56
Chapter 9	Elected Bishop of Canberra and Goulburn	60
Chapter 10	Resignation from the diocese	83
Chapter 11	On to Tasmania	89
Chapter 12	Retirement	96
Reflection		102
Appendix 1 Publications		103
Appendix 2 Other contributors		104

Foreword

About 15 years after his death, Bruce Stevens offers a memory of Owen Dowling. His book, *Harmony and Discord: The Life of Bishop Owen Dowling* comes as an account from a different time.

Most of Owen Dowling's life was lived in a world with at least residual sympathy and respect for the church. From the 1930s and 40s, when he went to church with his devoted Anglican father, through to involvements and explorations of adolescence, the church provided an encompassing environment for the young Owen Dowling and for many Australians.

In the 1950s, when Owen Dowling began to look seriously at the possibility of an ordained vocation, the churches in Australia were at a high point in terms of congregational attendance. Even into the 70s and 80s – as Stevens notes – several of the Anglican parishes where Owen Dowling was ministering had all-time record congregations.

When, as a bishop, Owen Dowling became a very public advocate for the ordination of women to the priesthood, his stance garnered national attention and sympathy. Even when he was surrounded by scandal, having been charged with soliciting for sex in a Bendigo Park, there was national interest and more than a little sympathy.

This was all before widespread allegations of child-sex abuse and cover-ups brought shame to the church and muted its voice. This was before an ideological assault on Christianity in Australia became the fashionable thing.

It was a different time. But it was not all good. Stevens offers only gentle commentary on the story. As he puts it, he prefers to let Owen sing solo. But the themes push gently through; the "boys club" of Anglican leadership, the monochrome and superficial approach to human sexuality, the institutional confidence that would later be exposed as betraying the abused.

Foreword

Stevens is careful to tell the Owen Dowling story as a whole. He does not allow those large public moments to dominate; the passionate advocacy for the ordination of women to the priesthood, the public scandal that led to his resignation.

Rather, he focuses on the man and his human contradictions, the harmony and the discord of a human life. Looking back from an era in Australian society when attitudes about human sexuality have profoundly shifted presents an easy temptation to speculate and theorise about how the Church in which Owen Dowling rose to prominence was also a church in which an integration and wholesome embrace of his own sexuality would always have been difficult.

Qualified as he undoubtedly would be to offer psychological insight on the human discord that was part of the Owen Dowling life-song, Stevens is restrained. He lets Owen Dowling comment on his own journey towards harmony, from that place of freedom that perhaps only came in retirement:

> We have to embrace the darker side of our experience as well as the brighter, lighter side, whereas sometimes in religion it is almost as if that is denied and we are meant to be ever so happy, joyful; no depressive thoughts and the immediate remedy of faith as it were...

Bruce Stevens brings the Owen Dowling story together in a sympathetic and light-touch way. He allows the character of a man of immense warmth and humanity shine through. And the discordant notes are there. It is harmony and discord.

Jeffrey Driver

The Rt Rev'd Dr Jeff Driver served in Canberra and Goulburn then later as Bishop of Gippsland and Archbishop of Adelaide (2005–2016).

Prelude

Owen Douglas Dowling was a public figure with a private life. Rarely are the two sides of a person in such sharp relief. But like a Bach fugue, which as an organist he played so well, the two counterpoint to form an interesting life.

Interesting? It is such a dull, over-worked word. But to know Owen was to engage with a person of great warmth, who was universally interested in others. The Anglican Church has produced more than its share of eccentric clergy. But Owen was not one of them. The same could be said of pompous Bishops. But he was not pompous. He was simply Owen.

After Owen's enthronement at St Saviour's Cathedral, Goulburn, I always called him Bishop. I recall kneeling to kiss his ring. I am not especially 'high church' in orientation, but somehow it seemed appropriate after such a grand event. In this book – my perspective on his life – he will be mostly Owen. I cannot keep referring to him with the formal the Right Reverend Owen Douglas Dowling, Bishop of Canberra and Goulburn (1983–1992). He would have cringed at the English honorific 'my lord'. He always answered to Owen. And this will continue in these pages.

A biography consists of a choir of voices. We are fortunate that Owen left 14 hours of interviews with *Canberra Times* journalist Mr Graham Downie, available on Trove.[1] And I also gladly acknowledge friends and colleagues of Owen – listed in Appendix 2 – who graciously provided other memories and stories that have enhanced the biography.

---

1 National Library of Australia, Trove see: nla.gov.au/nl.obj-207173143

Chapter 1

A child

Melbourne is somewhat 'youthful' for a major metropolis. Permanent settlement began in 1835 and barely two centuries have passed. Initially, it was the colonial capital of Victoria. The discovery of gold led to some prosperity and many elegant buildings. Steps towards a more sophisticated society were evident with the establishment of an art gallery, museum, library, botanic gardens, a telephone exchange, and cable cars from 1887. Progress indeed. The mood was vibrant with a rapidly growing population. But there was an economic 'bust' in 1891 which left many failed businesses and large numbers of unemployed. For a while, Melbourne was the capital of Australia (1901-1927). But it was not a happy time. Terrible losses were suffered in World War I and many of the young, surviving the war, died as a result of the Spanish Flu. A depression followed the Wall St crash in 1929. Any prosperity was 'patchy' and Melbourne had spreading areas of poverty. In 1930, the population grew to one million.

Just another birth in Melbourne? Yes, Owen was born 11 October 1934 to Cecil Gair Mackenzie Dowling and Winifred Hunter. He was 'bookended' by his older brother Ken and his younger brother Bryan. A neighbour asked a question which confused the young Owen, "Oh, did Bryan get found under a cabbage?" He could not quite picture the new baby being found under a cabbage. When Owen went to the private hospital to see Bryan, just born, there were not enough bassinets. He found Bryan in an open drawer. Perhaps the cabbage was not so ridiculous after all!

Cecil, his father, was initially a 'go-for' at the stock exchange and later a bank officer in the Royal Bank of Melbourne, which became the ES&A Bank.[2] While Cecil remained with the bank for all his working life, he was largely overlooked for promotion. He felt some resentment. Owen recalled his father showing him where he worked. He opened a drawer and there was a hand-gun, out-of-sight to respond if there was a robbery. It was a different era – perhaps reminiscent of the American 'Wild West'.

Cecil had close to a photographic memory which was evident when the history of the stock exchange was being written, he could remember 80% of the names of members including initials and provided them to the author in alphabetical order.

Cecil never forgave his father who had abandoned the family when he was a child. It was, apparently, in a fit of 'gold fever'. He went to live in a pub in Bendoc, where there is a picture of him on his 90th birthday with a cake.

Winifred was considered intelligent. She went to Methodist Ladies College on a scholarship. Later, she was employed at the Royal Bank and she met her future husband. Owen had a modest family life; his father was without a car until after he retired. Family walks were the primary source of leisure.

Cecil was unrelentingly negative in temperament. For example, he predicted that he would not live to see his 50th birthday. But he died at age 88, well past any estimate of 'average age at death' – then or now. Cecil would say, "Oh, we got married under a cloud". The 'cloud' was on a photo of the couple being married at St Bartholomew's, Burnley.[3] The photographer had put a thumb over the box Brownie aperture. Another 'cloud' was the death of Winifred's father, Mr William Hunter, days before the wedding, so the family was in mourning.

---

2 The ES&A Savings Bank Limited commenced on 29 September 1961. On 1 October 1970, "The Scottie" merged with the ANZ Bank Limited to become Australia and New Zealand Banking Group.

3 Owen was later the organist there when he attended university.

A child

Owen had pleasant memories of his childhood. His father would come home after work and, "I used to run down to him or go tearing down the hill in my little Bedford truck. That was my pedal car, which was a great companion of my childhood ... It was really one of my treasured childhood possessions. I would go tearing down the road and he would put down his brown case and take off his brown hat and I would get swept up into this brown-suited man's arms".[4] Owen also had a close emotional bond with his mother. "I think I used to tell her everything."

Owen spoke of his mother's generosity to those on the street. She would take meals to anyone sick. The family cared for the old Miss Oliver – 'Aunty' to the Dowling family. She would come for a meal once a week. And his parents were aware of anyone who needed assistance or nursing care. Visitors were always welcome.

Owen was raised in the church. "Well, my father was an extremely devoted Anglican and had been all his life. I was taken to church and Sunday school ... I didn't much like Sunday school. I thought it was very boring. I didn't like the kind of songs that they sang ... quaint old fashioned songs like *There's a Home for little Children above the bright blue Sky*." Sunday school seemed to focus on learning the prayerbook's catechism, 'What is your name?' Then after that, 'Who gave you this name?' He learnt to answer, 'My parents and godparents at my baptism, wherein I was made a member of Christ, a child of God and an inheritor of the Kingdom of Heaven'. Cecil was a man of apparent contradictions. He had some doubts. For example, he had no certainty of eternal life, but he would be the first to object if orthodoxy was not preached from the pulpit.

Owen was happiest in church. He possessed an aesthetic appreciation for the liturgy and colours of the church year. "I liked to like to sit down the front. This was at St James' Church, East

---

4 I have quoted extensively from the interviews. I have attempted to clean up the transcript and, where appropriate, express it in a more grammatical way, while keeping to the clear meaning. The transcript is readily available on-line.

Malvern, now called St James', Glen Iris[5] ... I loved to see what was going on. I suppose from earliest childhood, I was quite fascinated by the liturgy of the church and dressing up and so on. I always noticed what colours were being worn, the coloured stoles and the colours on the altar frontals and so on. I remember watching it all with great fascination." Perhaps a hint of vocation?

Owen had plenty of opportunity to attend church. Every Sunday Cecil was present at the 8 a.m. Holy Communion. He remained kneeling for the whole service. He was attracted to high rather than low church worship. Later, Owen described his background as middle-of-the-road Anglicanism. "We were certainly never ever taught that the world was made in six days, as some people fondly believe, or have difficulty with the biblical accounts of Creation or the literal character of certain Bible stories or whatever ... In the kind of religion in which I was brought up, church and sacraments and choir singing and organs and all that sort of thing was important ... We were taught the basics of the Christian faith but not in any fundamentalist kind of way." He used to listen carefully to sermons and appreciated those of the rector C. L. Moyes.

As a child, Owen would play church. He recalled, "Preaching a sermon to Aunty May, and to my young brother, Bryan, who were a kind of captive congregation ... I would dress up and lead the service and he would do various acolyte kinds of functions. Aunty May took this all very seriously. I can still see her sitting in the armchair. I would stand behind an armchair, which would be the pulpit, and I was dressed up in some sort of robe. I preached a sermon on The Good Samaritan". Aunty Flora's husband was a Presbyterian minister and, on occasion, Owen would attend his church in school holidays. Owen remained interested in the activities of clergy, but in his teenage years he became somewhat self-conscious and more discrete about being so 'churchy'.

---

5 There is a parish history of St James in the National Library of Australia. See: *The Story of the Church of St. James, Glen Iris*, (Carlton: Capitol Press, 1984?) 22 pages. The link is https://nla.gov.au/nla.cat-vn7091165

A child

Owen and his father would visit various places of worship. "We would do a bit of 'church crawling'. We would go into a Roman Catholic church here or an Anglican church there and this would lead to great discussions. I remember one day I was very deeply impressed by being taken by him to St Patrick's Cathedral ... then to St Peter's, Eastern Hill, which was opposite [across the road]. I can still remember the sense of awe that I had, going into St Peter's, and St Patrick's as well."

Owen discovered that he was a direct descendant of a Baptist minister. "To our shock and – horror, oh, horror is the wrong word I suppose – that the Dowlings were all descended from a Baptist minister. I can remember being quite surprised about this. Henry Dowling, my great, great-grandfather, came out to be the first Baptist minister in Van Dieman's land in 1834." There will be more about the family background in a later chapter on Owen's ministry in Tasmania.

Owen attended Gardiner Central School and later Melbourne High School. He was a bright child and ready for his primary education. Books were important in the family, and he was encouraged to read. He went to the 'bubs' class, or kindergarten, in the middle of 1939. He was asked to count to 100 which he did in the front of the class. He was assigned the duty of filling the inkwells. At the Central School, he recalled, "In the boys' toilet, there were all these marks where boys had tried to pee, [and] see who could pee the highest up the wall". Perhaps this is a good metaphor for professional ambition in the church?

Owen found that he had a natural talent in cricket. He could bowl both leg spin and top spin. He played house cricket at high school and, as an adult, played for a club team.

At school, he was considered a bit of a 'goody, goody'. He was academically able and some of his peers called him a 'swot', a derisive term for someone who studied. Ironically, Owen did not recall ever studying. With some gifted people intelligence carries them through school with little effort.

However, Owen was slow to learn 'the facts of life'. In fifth or sixth class, a school friend told him how babies were conceived.

Owen was quite sceptical. He responded, "No, I was told that when you wanted a baby you prayed to God, and it was an answer to prayer". Owen consulted his older brother, Ken, who discounted immaculate conception in favour of a more biological perspective.

Melbourne High School

There were some early spiritual highlights. Owen attended a performance of Stainer's *Crucifixion* when he was about 10 years old. No one in the family was available to go with him. He continued, "I can remember sitting there in open-mouthed astonishment while the different parts of the choir came in with: 'Fling wide the, fling wide the, fling wide the, fling wide the gates, for the Saviour waits to tread on His royal way' ... I can still get a feeling of excitement in me as I think of that music, and I wanted to be able to play it. Actually, several years later, I did play it when the choir was performing it". This musical experience was a moment of conversion. "I think that I really did open up my being to God and what God had done for me in Christ."

Owen had other moments. On holiday with his Aunty May, he was overwhelmed by the view from Bent's Lookout on Mt Buffalo. "It was probably about 6 a.m. and I was there entirely on my own. I can still remember that I shouted out words of praise to God. This was something that quite spontaneously came up from within my being. So I can't, these days, praise the God of Creation without thinking of an experience like that." It is easy to see the significance of such incidents in his spiritual development.

It was soon apparent that Owen had considerable leadership potential. When he was about 11 or 12 years old, he was encouraged by the Rev'd Cliff Moyes, the vicar of his church, to lead Lenten children's services. He was dressed up in a choirboy's cassock. Moyes also taught his confirmation class. At age 13, Owen was confirmed by Bishop McKie, an assistant bishop in the diocese of Melbourne. It was then that Owen started attending midweek services. "I can still remember the sense of mystery while kneeling at a small midweek communion in the early morning with the candlelight and with the priest in vestments and a sense of mystery about that which really drew me."

Surprisingly, he had a physical reaction. "I would get an erection. I remember being quite surprised and I couldn't work out the connection. I suppose I [now] understand that one could get an erection from any kind of excitement or stimulation. But I remember at the time being quite puzzled. I couldn't quite work out why religion would give one an erection."

There was a military tradition at his high school. Mr George Langley was the principal and he had previously held the rank of Brigadier. He became the principal after Major-General Ramsey. Owen was persuaded to join the school cadets. While he was not temperamentally suited to military service, it gave him an opportunity to go on camps and do various exercises. Later, as a young adult, Owen did National Service.

The school provided some religious instruction. The pupils assembled in the hall and either Archdeacon Schofield, the Anglican vicar from Christ Church, South Yarra, or Mr Martin, a Presbyterian minister at South Yarra Presbyterian, would speak. In relation to Mr Martin, "We used to call him Lou Lou because he couldn't say his r's properly, he used to say them like l's. So we called him Lou Lou Martin". The whole school of about a thousand boys would gather in the assembly for religious instruction. Owen remembered a message from Brigadier Langley. "One day, I think when the religious instructor didn't come, he gave us a long talk about being pure and how we must not get involved in committing sexual intercourse before we were married. I remember he gave us a very frank talk about this and how we had to keep ourselves pure for the woman that was waiting for us, that sort of idea. They also taught us then, I think, about French letters, the dangers of VD and so on."

In the equivalent of year 9, Owen joined the Waterloo House debating team. It was led by Barry Jones [a student 2 years older], who gained national fame as a Quiz Kid and later became a politician. The first debate was on the White Australia policy. Owen was being prepared for public speaking which would later figure prominently in his life.

Music was important in Owen's childhood. An early influence was Mrs Williams, the wife of the vicar who would play the harmonium at Sunday school. She would peddle away on a Mannborg organ while the children sang. "I still have memories of her teaching us *Who would True Valour See?*, the pilgrim hymn by John Bunyan. In verse two 'Who so beset him round with dismal stories', Mrs Williams [would get] us to sing 'dismal' with a tremendous emphasis."

Soon Owen was learning an instrument. At age 8, he started learning piano from Ms Violet Vernon. He soon mastered the basics and continued until he matriculated from high school. There was something of a musical tradition in his family. His maternal grandfather, William Hunter, was an organist and teacher of music. He was known as 'Professor' Hunter because of his teaching role. Mr Hunter was the organist at the Hawthorn Presbyterian Church and he taught both piano and organ. He was prominent in the Melbourne musical scene. He helped to found

A child

the Musical Society of Victoria. For a while, he was the city organist of Melbourne (in 1911). Owen's mother played the piano.

Owen found a place in the musical life of his local church. He did a piano item in the annual CEBS concert with parents in the audience. He also played in his teacher's annual concert of students. He recalled his first singing role at the school's speech night, in 4th class, performing *Old Man River* with his face blackened. In his final year of high school, he played the Beethoven Pathetique Sonata, First Movement, in the school assembly.

At age 14, he sang the bass part in the church choir. He found this both exciting and challenging. A year or so later, he had an opportunity to play the pipe organ in his local church. "I can still remember the thrill that I had, as a young man, just testing out various stops on the organ and finding out what sounds they made and playing some of my piano music, maybe Bach or Handel or whatever, what was suitable for the organ. I just took to it like a duck to water." In 1951, he became the organist at his church.

There was a dark aspect of Owen's childhood. He later shared with a confidant that he had been sexually abused by a close relative. Owen labelled his abuser the 'evil beast'. This is another aspect of what Owen struggled to come to terms with as a mature adult and being able to give himself in ministry.

Various trajectories emerged in Owen, as a child and adolescent, that were to continue throughout his adult life: musician, priest and eventual leader in the church. This can be seen in his life interests including classical music and the liturgical aspects of church life. His musical talents were recognised and developed, with opportunities to play before increasingly diverse audiences. He was becoming more confident in public speaking and leadership qualities were evident. What could be a better fit than the life he would soon assume?

Chapter 2

University

The University of Melbourne was founded by an act of parliament in 1853. It is the second oldest in Australia. Since 1872, a number of residential colleges have become affiliated with the university. The first was Trinity. The university is considered one of the six 'sandstone' schools and included in the Group of Eight which are research intensive. In 2022, the *Times Higher Education* ranked Melbourne University as first in Australia and 32nd in the world. It is a world class academic institution.

Owen was the first in his family to go to university. He had performed well in his matriculation with a first class honours result in Modern History, a second class in both English Expression and English Literature, a second class in Latin and a pass in General Maths. He had immersed himself in renaissance and reformation history. This was the result, in part, of discussions with his father about the Roman Catholic Church and his local vicar about the Anglican Church. He also talked theology with Mr Howe, his history teacher. Owen was accepted at Melbourne University where he majored in History and English, had a sub-major in Latin. He also took courses in Maths and Psychology.

Owen decided to pursue a career in teaching. "That was held before me as one of the ideals of my life, that I should be a teacher like my Aunty May. I was certainly given every encouragement to do that. In the end, I did go to university to do a secondary teacher's course. I suppose I had in the back of my mind that I would be able to switch across to the ministry if that was right for me."

He was attached to the Secondary Teachers' Training Centre (at Melbourne University). The centre provided extra support and tutorials. Students were paid a generous allowance, which was important to Owen because his parents were not affluent.

Owen's first essay impressed his history tutor. He was invited to do a four-year honours degree. He raised this with the head of the training centre but Owen was persuaded that a pass degree would be more useful in a teaching career. Later he had second thoughts. "In some ways, I have always regretted that, because I could have been quite a good historian. I have a very strong historical imagination and a lot of interest in history. I think I should have done an honours degree and maybe even gone on and done post-graduate work."

Owen benefited from good lecturers. He discovered the metaphysical poets John Donne and George Herbert. Their Christian perspective was influential to Owen's theological development. He also had exposure to the classical liberal arts tradition with classes in Latin and reading Livy, Cicero, Petronius Arbiter and Pliny.

Owen entered fully into what the university had to offer. This included various political, religious and musical societies. "I belonged to the choral society which took up one night a week and quite a few social activities and an annual trip away to the Intervarsity Choral Festival. I would go to every religious meeting that was advertised ... [the] Student Christian Movement or Evangelical Union or Newman Society and I would go and listen to the various speakers and even stay for some of the debates afterwards." The political meetings included the Labor Club, which was very left wing, the more moderate ALP Club, and the Liberal Club.

These years were a time of musical development. Owen became more skilled as an organist. After some frustration with the choirmaster at his local church, he became the organist of St Bartholomew's, Burnley. He sang with the Melbourne University Choral Society which included an annual trip to a choral festival.

He also engaged in various social activities including square dancing.

Owen was drawn into other musical activities. He became the organist for The Royal School of Church Music Demonstration Choir. This included organising a choral camp attended by choirboys from around Melbourne and across Victoria. The RSCM in Australia started to run summer schools in which Owen participated. His musical and church activities led to a clear sense of vocation.

Owen attended St Bartholomew's where Father Lyle McIntyre was the rector. Owen described him as "a rather dashing young priest who treated this whole work ... in a kind of romantic sort of way, copying the Anglo-Catholicism of some of the poorer areas of London, east London ... The idea was that you took colourful religion to the slums. McIntyre would go to the pub and we would have processions of witness along the streets. [Or] singing the Litany walking along the street on Good Friday or whatever, along the streets of Burnley. The church really flourished under his leadership". Owen became the organist and choir director of this working-class Anglo-Catholic parish.

This led to an experience that settled his sense of priestly vocation. In 1955, in his final year at the university, he was doing the Diploma of Education (DipEd) – the professional qualification required for teaching. A moment of realisation came when "Lyle had preached a sermon that had moved me very much, one Sunday night, where he told the story of a young man that he had met at Geelong Grammar, because he used to go down there and take a mission. This young man was in a very bad state, very upset state, and Lyle had been able to help him and bring some help and encouragement to him. I went home on the tram ... and I suddenly thought to myself: Why am I going through this charade of preparing to be a teacher, and telling everyone I was going to be a teacher, when if I really admitted the truth to myself, I really felt that I should be going into the ministry?"

Owen's sense of call was encouraged by Father Lyle. At age 21, he went on a private retreat for a few days at the Retreat House at Cheltenham. In this time of spiritual focus, he felt that God confirmed his call to the ministry. Later he was accepted by the examining chaplains as a candidate for the Diocese of Melbourne.

Owen's training to be a teacher was not a 'false-start'. While his future vocation lay in the ministry, not teaching, he gained a wide liberal arts education, training in how to communicate and he took further steps in leadership. Arguably it is also better to come to ministry having had experience in another profession. Nothing – as his life was to prove – was wasted.

Chapter 3

Life as a teacher

In Australia, at that time, there were two important trends that influenced a man or woman beginning a career in teaching. The demand for teachers increased after the World War II. The Commonwealth Government assumed a greater role in the financing of higher education from the States; and education was seen as important for economic growth. The 'baby boom' generation demanded a response. Later, during the early 1970s, there was a significant push to make tertiary education more accessible to working and middle-class people. In 1973, the Whitlam Labor Government abolished university fees.[6]

Owen benefited. He was able to attend the University of Melbourne and had support for his training. However, it came with 'payback'. He was bonded to teach for three years, which had the potential to delay his preparation for the ministry. And there was an additional obligation. Owen was in the National Service with a requirement to complete a three-month residential camp.

But this provided yet another musical opportunity. He joined the Concert Company which practised in the afternoons and presented a show at the end of the camp. He attended religious worship, both Anglican and Methodist, and engaged with the chaplains in theological discussions. He had no ambition for a career in the military. He remained at the private level in the anti-tank corps with the Melbourne University Regiment. At

---

6 "History of Higher Education in Australia" K12 Academics website.

camp, Owen managed to read Tolstoy's *War and Peace*. Perhaps appropriate?

In 1956, Owen began teaching at Castlemaine Technical School.[7] He lacked the support of a senior teacher in his discipline. So as a novice teacher, he began with face-to-face teaching of 35 hours a week and was responsible for organising the relief teaching staff. He enjoyed teaching the smaller classes in the senior school. The students were not especially literate, but Owen introduced them to Shakespeare's *Macbeth* and *Richard II*. He also taught poetry, and guided his students in how to write an essay.

Owen recalled having some difficulty with his middle classes. Students would ask him, "Sir, do you have a strap?" He was not inclined to rely on corporal punishment, having been told at university to reward students rather than punish them. However, they tested his resolve. He held out to Easter when, "I can remember getting so exasperated that I went into the machine shop of the tech and I said, 'Make me a strap' ... I started to use this strap, not very willingly I must admit. So I had a bit of a battle". It would appear that establishing discipline was essential for success in teaching, but – according to his daughter Mary – in his later years. he regretted using physical discipline.

Life in country Victoria agreed with Owen. "I was very stimulated. In Castlemaine, I threw myself into it with great zest. I acted in Agatha Christie's *Murder at the Vicarage*; I was the vicar. So the first time I ever put a clerical collar on was in that play. I was also in the church choir ... There was quite a good choir at Christ Church, Castlemaine." Unfortunately, Mr Keith Bottomley, the organist, had a breakdown that year.

Owen took over, later discovering – to his horror – that he was part of the reason. Apparently, Keith compared himself unfavourably to Owen. "I am a fairly multi-skilled kind of person and I have sometimes intimidated other people without realising ... I suppose I have pushed ahead doing things. I gave some recitals and

---

7 Until 1958, it was called the School of Mines.

I was enthusiastic about all the things that I did in church music, and I didn't realise that he felt very inadequate by comparison."

He was provided with other leadership opportunities. Owen became a lay-reader with the encouragement of the rector, the Rev'd Canon Dave Wallace. Owen would lead evening prayer and preach at Holy Trinity, Maldon, another historic township near Castlemaine. On occasion, Owen preached at Christ Church, Castlemaine. At this time, he was formally accepted as a diocesan candidate.

Owen reflected on his rural experience. "You move into the smaller pond of a country town and you are needed. So when I was in Castlemaine, or later on when I was the organist at Goulburn cathedral, in a country town, you do things that you wouldn't normally do in the city, like being asked to act in one of the local plays or I would be an accompanist. I can remember I had to play the piano at a fashion parade." He gained an appreciation for a more relaxed way of life and felt accepted in the local community.

Owen had been an assistant organist at St Peter's, Eastern Hill, while at university. Now he was offered the position of organist and choir master. This involved moving back to Melbourne, so Owen found a teaching position at Camberwell High. And later he taught at Northcote.

St Peter's Eastern Hill

Owen enjoyed the high church style of worship at St Peter's. "Ceremony, of course, was very important in such a place and you can imagine that the role of an organist was quite exciting. I would be sitting there, I would play before the service and then there would be five minutes of compulsory silence and then clang, clang, they would ring a bell out in the vestry, and in would come the high phalanx of clergy and servers, incense and the lot. They would all come in at quite a pace and I would extemporise on the organ. In would come the procession ... all with birettas on, which were taken off, and they would all genuflect and then they would go down and have the asperges, 'Thou shalt purge me, oh Lord, with hyssop'. We would be singing, the choir, and they would go down and slosh holy water on the people at the beginning of the service. There were lots of opportunities then during the service for the organist to extemporise, to fill in while different things happened, while the people got censed or whatever, and some very moving services indeed, beautiful services, and a very enthusiastic church full of people who wanted that kind of Anglo-Catholic style worship. [There were] quite a lot of young people, especially young men, who are attracted to that kind of religion and the dress-up."

It was at St Peters that Owen met his future wife, Ms Beverly Anne Johnston, who was an alto in the choir. She had been raised Presbyterian but found her way to St Peter's where she felt overwhelmed by the beauty of the services. Beverly had been dating the previous organist, but their relationship broke down by the time Owen arrived. After about six months, Owen asked her to go out. Eventually, he proposed (and was accepted).

Beverly knew that Owen was destined for the ordained ministry. Father Maynard married them in May 1958 at St Peter's. Owen recalled, "One amusing thing was that one of the choir members had to direct the choir because the choirmaster was getting married. But the choir were up in the gallery at the back of the church and we had arranged what they were going to sing and I can still remember as I walked out to the vestry after our marriage to sign the documents, with Beverly on my arm, I could hear the person conducting the choir give one note instead of a chord to the choir. I knew that the sopranos were going to pick up that one note, which was really the bass note of the chord, whereas they really needed to sing the dominant note of the chord. I could still think, 'It's going to go wrong, it's going to go wrong'. Sure enough, it did. The sopranos finished up about a fifth higher than they should have been, and they all had to start again, so that amused me".

Beverly was well read in literature and poetry. Owen noted, "She had a kind of melancholic streak in her and she was very drawn to the darker side of human experience ... People would often confide in her, with their pains and troubles, and I think that that was partly because of her own slightly melancholic personality".

She also enjoyed acting. When he began courting her, Beverly was in *Under Milkwood* by Dylan Thomas. Owen described her as "a great person, full of fun and full of interesting stories and always saw the funny side of things and we had a very good companionship together". Beverly had trained as a librarian, having worked previously at the State Library, but then she went to the Olympic Tyre and Rubber Company in Footscray. This was not a position she enjoyed.

After their marriage, Owen returned to teaching at Northcote High. Soon he began to study theology. Beverly was soon pregnant with Timothy.[8] "The only thing she complained about was that having the baby in her womb made her sing sharp, sort of pushed up her diaphragm." The couple's plans had to change. Owen had to continue teaching, which he did half-time, while attending classes in theology at Trinity. His schedule became full, with classes in the morning, teaching in the afternoon, and then back to St Peter's to prepare for choir practice. Or he would go to the library at Trinity and do some work in the late afternoon and then stagger home. He recalled learning Greek with Dr Leon Morris in classes shared with Ridley students.

Already, we see Owen adapting to an unusual pace of life. He managed to pack everything into a hectic schedule with teaching, doing theology and directing music at St Peter's church. He did all this while settling into married life and starting a family. He may have attempted to excuse this as a temporary phenomenon, since almost every busy person tries that out on long suffering spouses, but it would have been a 'false promise' as his later years in ministry were to prove.

---

8 Timothy John, who at the time of the interview was the principal trombone player in the Residency Orchestra of The Hague.

Chapter 4

Ordained for ministry

What was the beginning of the Anglican Church in Melbourne? Various dates have been suggested. Was it the first prayer book service (30 April 1837)? Or the appointment of the first resident clergyperson (Rev'd J. C. Grylls in 1838)? Or the laying of the foundation stone for the first church St James (9 November 1838)? Or the appointment of the first Bishop of Melbourne (Rt Rev'd Charles Perry, 1846)? The diocese was separated from the Diocese of Australia by letters patent on 25 June 1847. It included the cities of Melbourne and Geelong with some more rural areas. If we 'fast forward' a hundred years, the Diocese of Melbourne was undergoing changes in the 1950s. A survey of the Diocese indicated potential growth areas. The diocesan program 'Forward Move' was launched and led by Archdeacon Geffrey Sambell. This included increases in expenditure on clergy training, and the funding of pastoral initiatives including new parishes, hospital and institutional chaplaincies. Melbourne is a diverse diocese with the three traditions of Evangelical, Liberal and Anglo-Catholic all well represented. Sir Frank Woods was the Archbishop from 1957 to 1977.

Owen was ordained deacon in 1960. Since he had a university degree, the two year Licentiate in Theology (LTh) was considered sufficient for his theological preparation. He was made deacon and received a placement at Sunshine with the vicar, the Rev'd

Bruce Reddrop.[9] Owen was in Sunshine for two years (1961-1962). At that time, there were 63,000 people living in the housing commission area of Sunshine and Deer Park. It was a ministry with considerable demands, and this provided some obstacles to Owen completing the last few units of the degree. Later, he said that the distractions of ministry cost him a first-class honours in theology.

St Paul's Cathedral, Melbourne

---

9 Reddrop later became the director of Anglican Marriage Guidance, eventually called by another name, but after Sunshine he devoted his time to counselling and marriage counselling.

Tragedy was to hit the Reddrop's. Helen, their six year old daughter, died of leukaemia. Owen had to assume far more responsibility than was normally expected of a newly minted deacon. He later reflected, "I suppose, in a way, that has been my life. When I look back, I can see that I have had a lot of responsibility thrust upon me, almost too quickly sometimes". He was ordained priest in March 1961.

Such pressures were to continue. At the end of this placement, he expected a second curacy, but when he went into the archbishop's office (and after a limp English hand-shake), he was greeted, 'Good afternoon, vicar'. Owen was appointed to West Heidelberg (1962-1965), another large housing commission area of Melbourne. This included the Olympic village. When Owen left 3½ years later, he heard that his position had been offered, and declined, by 33 clergy! But he was so junior that it was not 'offered' – he was appointed without discussion.

Owen remembered going to West Heidelberg with Beverly in a small Austin A40. They drove around the streets – a kind of wilderness – with low socio-economic house upon house and street upon street. At the time, it was the largest such area in Melbourne.

There was to be no rest for Owen. The parish had three churches which included St Phillip's, which had been an older branch church established from the main church at Heidelberg, and St Columba's in the Olympic village, which met in the Olympic hall with a Sunday school, and St Peter's, a small church at West Ivanhoe. Each had Sunday services, so Owen was given a full-time curate, the Rev'd Barry Smith, who was paid by the diocese. The rector that followed him, the Rev'd Tassie Pappas, said that Owen was highly regarded by the parishioners, when he left the parish, and the worship was of a high standard.

St Phillips had a tradition of hymn singing. Owen commented, "I suppose ever since then it has become one of the mainlines of my life, to be concerned about teaching people to sing hymns and psalms. We did it so well that the ABC broadcast a parish Eucharist with congregational singing. The ABC came out and we were held up as a sort of example to others of corporate congregational worship".

The family expanded with the birth of Matthew in January 1961. Matthew was hard to settle because he was born in the middle of a heatwave. Owen would often get up from bed to attend to his needs. "I can still remember sitting in my study at Deer Park, which had a gas fire in it. It was a small room, and it was a good place to dry the napkins and I recall sitting in the middle of all these steaming napkins doing my theology, trying to get myself educated." It was a small, three-bedroom housing commission house with a lounge room, also used for parish meetings. There was no entrance area; everyone had to go through the living room to eventually arrive at the study. The Dowling family life was exposed to all who entered. When Mary was born in 1964, it resulted in significant overcrowding – 'there was no room in the inn'.

The assistant bishop of the diocese was approached to provide more suitable housing. However, he was a single man and made a bizarre suggestion to Beverly. "Tell Owen to get a caravan and put it in the drive and you can use that as extra accommodation." Owen reflected, "I came back to an enraged wife. She was pacing up and down saying, 'I'm not going to live in a bloody caravan'. I suspect that such experiences were typical of clergy life before conditions became standardised!"

Life in the parish was not short of challenges. Liberty Parade was a street in West Heidelberg. Most of the local criminals seemed to live on this street. He would read in the papers about another person sent to prison and inevitably the address of the convicted would be on Liberty Parade. Ironically, Liberty Parade! He would visit families and "I learnt the art of ministry and I learnt to mix it with all kinds of people in all kinds of situations. I visited gaols. I was a probation officer, so I used to have to go and do reports for some of the young offenders to the courts and have them report to me ... [it] introduced me into the life of the area".

There were other social issues. Generally at that time, couples wanted to be married in a church. But pregnancy was not unusual for the soon-to-be-wife. This was not usually admitted, but "You would open the front door and find this girl standing there clutching her stomach and she would say, 'We want to get married'. You had to think of discreet ways of asking them, 'Are you being forced to be married or is this your own free will'?"

Owen thrived in stressful situations. But he was unprepared for some of roles thrust upon him in his first few years of ordained ministry. And this pattern of being 'thrown in the deep-end' was to repeat again and again. He met expectations by coping, not complaining, and then excelling. Not a bad life script.

Chapter 5

The cathedral in Goulburn

Goulburn was named by surveyor James Meehan after Henry Goulburn, Under-Secretary for War and the Colonies. Governor Lachlan Macquarie ratified it. The colonial government made land grants to free settlers, including Hamilton Hume, with settlement beginning in 1820. Goulburn was established in 1833.

Goulburn holds the unique distinction of being proclaimed a city on two occasions. The first, unofficial, proclamation was claimed by virtue of Royal Letters Patent issued by Queen Victoria on 14 March 1863 to establish the Diocese of Goulburn. It was a claim made for ecclesiastical purposes, as it was required by the traditions of the Church of England. The Letters Patent also established St Saviour's Church as the Cathedral Church of the diocese. This was the last instance in the British Empire in which Letters Patent were used in this way.

However, under the authority of the *Crown Lands Act 1884*, Goulburn was officially proclaimed a city on 20 March 1885, removing any lingering doubts about its status. Such questions did not hinder the development of Goulburn as a regional centre. There was considerable local pride in the court house (completed in 1887) and other public buildings. The city became a centre for wool, and eventually some industry.

The Diocese of Goulburn was the second to be carved out of the Diocese of Sydney after the Diocese of Newcastle. One of the grandest buildings was St Saviour's Cathedral, designed by Edmund Thomas Blacket. It was completed in 1884 and the tower added a hundred years later. Originally, the diocese extended from the south coast of NSW to the South Australia border, sparsely inhabited and daunting for any ministry on horse-back!

Owen was not finished with rural life. He noticed an advertisement for precentor and organist at St Saviour's Cathedral in Goulburn.[10] This was a clergy role that drew on his musical ability. As a student, Owen had visited the Gothic Revival style cathedral and was impressed by its architectural merit. Owen's application got the attention of Dean King and Bishop Clements. Soon he was on his first plane flight (from Melbourne to Canberra). When he arrived, he found the cathedral organ to have deteriorated and his sense of 'call' included the restoration of the organ. He accepted the position.

He and Beverly looked at housing options and chose 10 Church Street – an old schoolhouse, built in the 1840s. It had a schoolroom which became the lounge room, and the schoolmaster's main room or the master bedroom, and it had two other smaller rooms as well. While it was reasonably large, it was poorly heated, draughty, had rising damp and bats! In 1965, Goulburn had the coldest winter on record.

---

10 See the history of the cathedral by William C. Stegemann, *An Ornament to the City: A History of the Cathedral Church of St Saviour, Goulburn, 1874-1988* (1989). https://catalogue.nla.gov.au/Record/2244763/

The cathedral in Goulburn

St Saviour's Cathedral, Goulburn

It was a difficult time for Beverly. She lost her father, Mr Max Johnston, in Melbourne in November of that year. She felt alone in a new city. And Owen –rarely there because of parish work.

In contrast, Owen remembered living in Goulburn with some fondness. His duties began at an early hour. "In the mornings, I used to get up to go over to the cathedral for 7 o'clock church each morning. They had a daily service, so it was an early rise, but the beautiful crisp, frosty mornings – I can still remember them – and hearing the Southern Highlands Express, which would leave the Goulburn railway station at 10 to 7 each morning. I would hear the engine get up steam and out the train would go. In fact, it remained as a steam train." He also recalled that, after a fall of snow, his children built a life-sized snowman. Owen delighted in the opportunities of a country town.

Owen was soon burdened with a heavy schedule. This was, by now, a familiar experience to him in ministry. "My average Sunday was extremely heavy at Goulburn Cathedral. I would go to a church that was in a place called City View, which was up in the housing area. I would go there at 7 a.m. and take a little Communion service and then I would go back to the cathedral and assist with the 8 o'clock cathedral service, which in those days had a very big congregation and they always had a few hymns, so I would slip on to the organ and play some hymns and assist with the administration of communion. Then I would go at 9.15 a.m. to either East Goulburn or South Goulburn, again little churches, which had been founded back in the days when people didn't have cars, and everybody had to walk to their local church ... then I would come back to the cathedral. It had to be a very short service, and then I would do the Sunday school ... which was in the cathedral at 10 a.m. Then at 11 o'clock there would be the main morning service at the cathedral, Morning Prayer or Sung Eucharist, and the choir would be on deck for that. Then we would go to the St Saviour's Children's Home ... every week, Beverly and I and our three children went up to the children's home and had lunch with the girls." But his day was not over. "Then in the evening I would play for Evensong and the choir would sing but the normal practice was that I would preach."

The Children's Home provided a sense of community. At times, the staff helped Owen and Beverly with their three young children. Owen became the director of the St Saviour's Children's Home choir, and they would sing at various events in Goulburn. Soon things became even more hectic. "On Easter Day 1966, I was setting up my papers in the pulpit before the service and Dean King came up and he had a great pile of papers in his hand which he put into my hand. He was an abrupt sort of person. He really didn't like talking about himself. He said, 'Here, take these. I have got to go under the knife and I don't know whether I'll be back'." The Dean had been given a diagnosis of stomach cancer and, as he suspected, he did not recover. Later, Owen would conduct the Dean's funeral service, comfort his family and assume his many duties at the cathedral.

A cathedral is like an actor playing many parts: naturally, it is a large church building, hosting diocesan events such as ordinations and synod services; but equally it is a parish church with normal routines. Bishop Clements provided an assistant priest, but Owen was in charge of running the cathedral for the next nine months.

It was only natural that he harboured some ambitions. He was hoping that he might be appointed Dean but, in 1967, a more senior clergyperson, Canon Harold Palmer, was given the role of vice-dean and canon residentiary. Owen returned somewhat reluctantly to being his assistant and the precentor.

Random things occurred in the life of the cathedral. "One Evensong, when we had just got to the Magnificat, and suddenly the dean's dog, whose name was Rex, had a fight with Fluffy, who was the dog from the St Saviour's Children's Home. They had a fight in the middle of the aisle of the cathedral right in the middle of the Magnificat." Such interruptions seem to have been accepted. Owen became involved in Goulburn's local music scene which included ecumenical choirs. He also taught Latin at the local Presbyterian Ladies College.

Owen was getting restless at the Cathedral. He could see the potential of this ministry from his year-in-charge. He thought Dean King had overstayed his time and, "Harold was inclined to be very formal, a sort of strict Anglo-Catholic. He mishandled people quite a lot. I remember an occasion with [Mr] Don Wheeler who was a sidesman at the cathedral. It was a synod service and the back door of the cathedral kept banging open and shut; it was a cold and windy night. I think it was an evening service, probably a synod Evensong service. Harold walked up to Don and said, 'Shut the door', like that, you see, and Don took no notice and went on sorting the books or whatever he was doing. Harold said to him, 'Shut the door', and Don said to him, 'Shut the bloody thing yourself.' I think that was just about the last that Don saw of serving with Canon Palmer".

The functions of diocesan administration gradually shifted to Canberra. There was some resentment in Goulburn, as Owen noted. "I think that Goulburn got a bit down in the dumps about itself. It was quite noticeable to me and Beverly when we moved to Wagga at the beginning of 1968, that there was a whole different spirit there. Wagga Wagga was a lot more go-ahead and more positive about itself, because it was the gateway to the Riverina ...

and it's survived well economically." Clearly Owen was open to a change in ministry.

In Owen's interview about his time in Goulburn, we get a rare glimpse of his ecclesiastical ambitions. Every Anglican clergyperson is aware of the 'pecking order' in a diocese. Owen hoped that he might be appointed dean, but it would have been unusual to jump from assistant priest to such a senior diocesan role, even a priest as successful in ministry as Owen. I doubt if such a 'lift in status' would have been seriously considered by the Bishop. But even if for some reason he was favoured in this way, there would have been a negative reaction from clergy in the diocese. Owen needed a few years preparation as rector of a large parish, but at least for a time he was 'centre stage' in the mother church of the diocese.

Chapter 6

For a time ... in Wagga

The first European explorer to visit the Wagga area was Captain Charles Sturt in 1829. Charles Tompson, an emancipated convict, was the first settler. In 1832, he established himself with his family on the north bank of the river. Other settlers followed, to squat on the land illegally. By 1836, the colonial government regulated their tenure with a licensing scheme. Later, with an increasing population and some prosperity, Wagga and the surrounding district was subject to the criminal activities of several infamous bushrangers, including Mad Dog Morgan and Captain Moonlite. In the 20th century, Wagga Wagga continued to grow and, on 17 April 1946, it was proclaimed a city. The suburbs of Turvey Park, Mount Austin and Kooringal were established with over 1,200 Housing Commission homes.

There was a growing need for a centre of ministry in the south of the city. St John's, the original church in the area, assumed responsibility. In February 1948, Archdeacon Stanley West suggested building in Turvey Park. Later, Archdeacon Bob Davies had buildings transported from Kapooka Army Base. The first service was conducted on Christmas morning 1955. St Alban's in Kooringal had also been part of St John's when it was established in 1958. It was served by junior clergy appointed to St John's church. In 1969, the parish of South Wagga Wagga was established with Kooringal later breaking off to form at parish in 1979. Money was raised to build a rectory and parish hall for St Paul's. There was a strong connection with the Wagga Wagga Teachers College providing trainees to help with the Sunday school.

Owen shared his restlessness with the diocesan bishop. The Right Rev'd Ken Clements was approachable and Owen liked his warm, pastoral style. The possibility was raised of becoming the rector of the new parish of South Wagga. This included St Paul's Church, South Wagga, and St Alban's, Kooringal. However, the idea was not warmly received. The three church representatives on the clergy appointment committee were evangelical. They raised an objection because Owen had a reputation for being an Anglo-Catholic. Bishop Clements thought of a way around this obstacle. He appointed Owen priest in charge, hoping that he could later be appointed rector. He was inducted to the parish of South Wagga Wagga on 1 February 1968.

Once the people got to know Owen, in just a few weeks, the laypeople approached the bishop to have him appointed rector. He remained there five years from 1968 to 1972. The parish history noted that he was remembered for his enthusiasm.[11]

Owen recalled an instance of God's provision. "I remember when we moved in, a funny little event happened. Beverly and I were flat strapped. We didn't have any money. There was a gap in the pay arrangements, and I think I had run out of money altogether, so we sat there wondering what we were going to do to tide us over until I got paid by the new parish. I think I said, 'Oh well, the Lord will provide', and no sooner had I said 'The Lord will provide', there was a knock on the door and the previous occupant of the house, who was the curate at Saint John's [the main church in Wagga], said, 'Oh, I have come to pay you the money for my portion of the electricity bill'."

Owen took the initiative in relating to the evangelicals at St Paul's. There was a large Bible study with 30 or 40 young people coming late Sunday afternoon, then staying for a fellowship tea and evening prayer before going to house groups. Owen played the organ and sometimes had people back to the rectory. He also

---

11 Ian Grant, *Unity in Diversity: The Story of the Anglican parish of South Wagga Wagga* (Published by the Anglican parish of South Wagga Wagga, 2018), 25.

had vigorous discussions on whether certain passages of the Bible should be taken as literal.

The Rev'd Canon Kevin Stone was a student at the Teachers College and an evangelical in the Sydney tradition of churchmanship. He was later ordained served in a number of parishes in the diocese. He described Owen's preaching as very engaging, teaching from the Scriptures with clear application. Kevin would often note in his diary that he heard a good evangelical sermon from Owen. He also recalled that Owen had a talent for remembering names.[12] Humorously, he recalled that one of the rumours circulating in the parish at the time of Owen's appointment was that he was in the Legion of Mary!

St Paul's grew in attendance. The 8 o'clock service was full every Sunday and had about 120 communicants. Extra seating was brought in. There was an increase in the other services with about 50 or 60 coming to the evening service, which adopted a more contemporary style of worship including choruses. Hymns with traditional words would be sung with a modern tune. With some amusement Owen remembered, "We used to sing *The Lord's my Shepherd* to the tune of *The House of the Rising Sun*, which is, of course, rather funny when you think about it, using a song about a brothel for good pious evangelicals to sing their hymn". The other worship centres – Kooringal and Lake Albert – also increased in attendance. Soon there was enough money to employ a curate.

The parish history noted that Owen demonstrated his pastoral gifts through a variety of initiatives, including a visitation scheme to maintain contact with all the people listed on the parish roll. An area warden and street wardens were appointed to facilitate improved pastoral care. The parish also produced a paper *The South Wagga Anglican*. It was not surprising that Owen organised musical events including concerts. He instituted a monthly healing service and the occasional service of the Order of St Luke. He

---

12 Later, Kevin remembered the influence of Owen in the ministry of healing. Kevin established a chapter of the Order of St Luke when he was rector of Cooma (2000-2004).

supported a variety of Anglican organisations such as the Young Anglicans, Sunday school, St Paul's choir, Church Women's Union and the Ladies Evening Fellowship. One of the older parishioners, Betty McCulloch, recalled his sermons as being steeped in practical examples of Christian living.

The parish benefited from Owen's musical talents. St Pauls had a good choir with Beverly as a member. Practices were in the rectory, which avoided the necessity of a baby-sitter. It was important to Owen to maintain his musical skills. "I realised that if you don't actually do music, if you are a musician, several things happen. One is you go rusty and in the end you can't do it ... The other thing is that people forget that you can actually play, and so you don't get asked to do things. I made a resolution then, just as I went to Wagga Wagga, that if anyone asked me to do anything musically, I would say yes, no matter how inconvenient." He was determined to put on an organ recital, at least once a year, and play something new. When Alan Walker ran his Mission to the Nation, Owen played a Hammond organ in the Wagga Civic Centre. Owen was also on the national committee for the Royal School of Church Music.[13] The Carmelites had a monastery in Wagga and Owen would spend quiet time there. He participated in a range of ecumenical endeavours, including the training of religious education teachers.

In Wagga, Owen embarked on what was to become a lifetime project. In late 1967, a group of Presbyterians, Methodists and Congregationalists were thinking about developing a hymnbook. Owen was asked to be the Anglican observer. In 1968, the committee made steps to develop an Australian hymnbook. Over the next 32 years, Owen made a huge contribution to this project.[14] The ecumenical *The Australian Hymn Book* was published in 1977.[15] Internationally, it also became an influential model for denominational cooperation in hymnbooks. *Sing Alleluia*, a supplement of 100 hymns, came out in 1987. *Together in Song* was

---

13 This committee met in Sydney.
14 He attended meetings in Sydney and Melbourne.
15 This book is one of the 'best sellers' in Australia, with over a million copies sold.

published in 1999 and included hymns from the Lutheran and Church of Christ traditions. Owen wrote the hymn 'I set the Lord before my eyes' which is number 643 in *Together in Song*.

His editorial activities led to various opportunities. For example, later after *Together in Song* was launched, Owen recalled, "St Peter's Cathedral, Adelaide was absolutely full of singers. We had circulated all the choirs of Adelaide and they had all come along with their prepared music, having learnt some of the hymns from the book and I spoke about the hymns that were sung. We had about six choirs performing. We had people filling the whole cathedral and up into the gallery as well. So we had about 1,000 people singing and it was really one of the most uplifting experiences which I have ever had, ever taken part in, as far as worship is concerned and music is concerned. It was really thrilling".

In Wagga, Owen became friends with Ms Barbara and Mr Dick Helm. Barbara was involved with the Order of St Luke. With Owen, they attended the chapter which met in Junee and Coolamon. Later, Owen established a chapter in Wagga. He had a lasting interest in the healing ministry.[16] He noted, "The Order of Saint Luke is a very good organisation. It is ecumenical and international, so you are introduced into a fellowship of people across the churches. It also has a sensible approach to healing where

---

16 When Owen became a chapter chaplain, "I was often in the position of having to lead in prayer and ministry. This required some stepping out in faith with few visible means of support. I likened it at the time to walking out on a plank and diving in ... I did learn to be bold and direct in my praying and to listen to what the Spirit was saying, and as well to heed pictures that came to mind as I prayed for particular people. Time and time again people experienced blessing and healing and being known and cared for by God". See *Channels of Healing: Studies for the People of God* (Wantirna, Victoria: Order of St Luke the Physician. 2002) with 30 study chapters. At the end of this book is an address "Caution, Boldness, Presumption: Our Need for a Discerning Spirit" (p. 64). He also recalled a significant experience in his ministry with Roy Parsons (London Healing Mission) "It moved me to tears when I saw Jesus healing through him ... I was weeping because of what I believed about Jesus, a reality 2000 years ago, now I saw happening before my eyes" (p. 64).

it is not so much that you always have to expect a physical healing but the whole idea of wholeness in body, mind and spirit is there".

The Rev'd David Clark was appointed as curate in South Wagga, serving with Owen for three years. He came from an Evangelical background. They said morning and evening prayer together which established a prayerful foundation for their ministry together. David was impressed with Owen's expository preaching from the Bible. He also recalled a later comment by Owen, when he was the diocesan bishop, that the Word of God had meant more to him in recent years.

Owen remained in Wagga for five years. The family thrived. Beverly got a part-time job at the Wagga library and participated in a Shakespeare reading group. Tim started to play the trombone. He was soon in a school jazz band. Owen jogged (until he had a heart attack in 1989) and he continued to play cricket – on one occasion making a century in Kooringal. He was awarded a dozen bottles of Cottee's lemonade for the 'ton'. The family became 'rich' in relationships. A neighbour's child would call in, "Whenever Susan got upset, she would come into the kitchen and she would say, 'A bickie would help, Mrs Dowling'. That was one of the things we remembered in our family life: 'A bickie would help'".

Owen was becoming more prominent in the diocese. He was on Bishop in Council and joined the leadership team. Years later, on one of his first formal occasions as diocesan bishop, Owen opened the new church of St Paul's (February 1982). It was designed by Mr Bryan Dowling, his younger brother, who was a prominent architect.

We can see another aspect of Owen in his ministry in Wagga Wagga. While he retained his Anglo-Catholic identity, he was flexible in his style of ministry. He could engage with believers across the Anglican spectrum – most surprisingly with Evangelicals (who are often hard-to-please) – middle Anglicans including liberal, and, increasingly, the charismatics with his emphasis on the healing ministry. Naturally, he was appreciated by anyone who valued musical talent and had a refined sense of liturgy. Like St Paul, he could be 'all things to all people' (1 Corinthians 9:22).

Chapter 7

St John's, Canberra

The Canberra area was first explored in the 1820s. Joshua Moore received the first grant of land: 2000 acres, roughly covering what is now Civic and including much of the northside to Dickson. Decades later, this largely rural area assumed a greater importance.

At about the turn of the 20th Century, everyone agreed that Australia needed a national capital. The two contenders were Sydney, as the oldest city, and Melbourne, as the largest city. Canberra was the compromise. The Federal Capital Territory was created in 1911 (the land donated by NSW). Walter Burley Griffin won the competition to design the capital, and, with the help of his architect wife, guided the development of this soon-to-be city.

Canberra was officially named by Lady Denman in 1913. The first residential blocks were sold in 1924 and the city grew substantially after World War II when many of the federal departments in Melbourne finally moved to Canberra. The Australian National University began as a research institute in 1946.

The wealthy merchant Robert Campbell gave a grant of land to establish St John the Baptist Church. He was the owner of the Duntroon estate. Campbell chose the site, with construction beginning in 1841 and the church consecrated 1845.[17] The Campbell family were substantial benefactors of the church paying

---

[17] In consultation with Bishop William Broughton, Bishop of Australia; Eds Kevin Stone and Charles Body, *Deep and Lasting Foundations: Parishes of the Anglican Diocese of Canberra and Goulburn*, (Broughton Books, 2013), 82.

half of the cost with the rest paid by the New South Wales government. From 1865 to 1870, the sandstone tower, designed by architect Edmund Blacket, was built. The graveyard is significant since the headstones record early settlers as well as later arrivals in the early years of the national capital. By the 1970s and 1980s, St John's became a city church with parishioners drawn from across Canberra. The church was becoming more widely known outside the ACT, as a result of visits by members of the royal family.[18]

The Right Rev'd Cecil Warren followed Clements as the next bishop of Canberra and Goulburn. He recognised Owen's many talents and presented him with a number of attractive choices for his next ministry. There were three options: rector of St Johns, Canberra, rector of St Paul's, Manuka, and Dean of Wangaratta. Owen was now on the ecclesiastical 'fast track'. He chose St John's.

Owen met with two of the three parish representatives. There was some concern about his involvement in the healing ministry. However, his responses to their questions were satisfactory. In October 1972, the Dowling family moved to Canberra.[19] He was to be the rector of St John's for the next 9 years. In October 1974, he was appointed Archdeacon of Canberra.

---

18 See also Alf H. Body, *Firm still you stand*, (Canberra: St John's Parish Council, 1986).
19 In 1971, there were 146,000 people living in Canberra.

The first church in Canberra, St John's, in the suburb of Reid

Owen explained why the ministry at St John's was so demanding. "It is a small church, yet it has a large congregation drawn from all over Canberra. I think at one stage we had people on our parish list that were in every suburb in Canberra. So, if you visited people, you had to visit all over Canberra. There were a lot of weddings, being a popular place, so it meant there was a lot of marriage preparation ... Not only did you have a number of services[20] but you had a variety of services in what each particular congregation preferred their way of worship. I always thought St John's was a bit like a religious smorgasbord. People could come and select what they wanted." There were additional centres in Hall and Sutton, and occasional services on historic rural properties. There were two curates on the staff and a secretary in the office.[21]

---

20 There was 7 a.m., 8 a.m., 9.30 and 11a.m. with 7 p.m. Five services a Sunday.
21 It seems likely that Owen was rector when St Johns had the most people attending worship, Alf Body (1986) noted that the number of communicants declined each year after 1981, but were higher than 10 years before, p. 289. The annual number was at the highest – 20,250 – in 1980 in the history of St John's.

Owen was not a traditional clergyman in the mould of his predecessor Archdeacon Fred Hill. In his first pastoral letter to the congregation, he stated that his priority was 'to equip God's people for work in his service'. He also mentioned 'speaking and healing in the name of Christ'. Beverly also differed from Fred's wife Mary. She began to help, on a voluntary basis, at St Mark's, a theological library. This provided a useful excuse to avoid tedious women's meetings in the parish. Beverley had interests in poetry reading and the creative arranging of flowers.[22]

St John's was to prove a hard time for her. Beverly and Owen had only been in the parish a year when she began to receive poison pen letters. "These nasty little letters came to Beverly with a little bit of typing in the middle of the blank sheet of paper and it was things like, 'You don't care about your husband. You only like the limelight'." As a young teenager, their daughter Mary received 'sympathy' cards on her birthday from this person, saying that she needed sympathy to have such a mother![23] Beverly sank into depression and was twice admitted to Canberra Hospital. Owen observed, "The voice of the poison pen letters was like a thousand voices to her." The police were called but the writer was never identified. The letters persisted and later some were sent to Mrs Warren, the Bishop's wife, and after 1993 Owen's second wife Gloria was to receive a number. This is a reminder that there is a dark and ugly side to church life which often bears down most heavily on clergy and their families.

As Archdeacon of Canberra, Owen became a confidant of Bishop Warren, along with the Rt Rev'd Neville Chenoweth, the assistant bishop. When both bishops were away, for example

---

22 Owen mentioned that Beverly gave him feedback on his sermons, to be more decisive and not say 'on one hand...' in *Channels of Healing: Studies for the People of God*, Wantirna, (Victoria: Order of St Luke the Physician, 2002) with 30 study chapters. At the end of this book is an address "Caution, Boldness, Presumption: Our Need for a Discerning Spirit" (p. 64).
23 It would appear that the poison pen letters were from someone who knew the family very well.

attending the Lambeth Conference, Owen became the administrator of the diocese. Effectively, he was third in the diocesan 'pecking order'. He made a mark on the diocese by helping to establish Bishopthorpe as a centre for spirituality.[24] It had previously been the home of early bishops in the diocese. Later, it was occupied by a religious order, the Community of the Ascension. In their time – of about 20 years – the chapel used seven times a day for services. After some restoration, retreats began.

While Owen was at St John's, he was a member of Bishop-in-Council and a member of the Property Trust. When divisions were created, Owen became convenor of the committee that established new parishes in the diocese and promoted stewardship. Mr Robert Arthur, a prominent layperson in the diocese, recalled being on Bishop-in-Council at this time. Bishop Cecil was proposing to dissolve a formal covenant with the Uniting Church. This would have affected his home parish of Holy Covenant, Aranda. Robert prepared a clear argument against the Bishop's proposal. When he finished speaking, he heard Owen from the other end of the table saying quietly, but firmly, "Hear, hear!". Robert was the only member questioning the Bishop's action and he appreciated this support, knowing that it took some courage for a senior clergyman to openly disagree with his Bishop. Clearly, Owen was no sycophant.

Owen continued with the Order of St Luke. About a month after he arrived at St John's, he was taking the Sunday evening service and debated with himself about whether he should call people forward for healing. It was a service with many young adults. Owen mulled over this while delivering the sermon and the long hymn that followed. "I kept thinking, 'I should call people forward, I should call people forward', and I was getting quite aggravated about it. So in the end I said to myself, 'Well, I'll do it'".

A hymn had been sung earlier in the service, *Oh my Saviour lifted from the Earth for me, Draw me in thy Mercy nearer*

---

24 See the history of Bishopthorpe, Garnett Webster and Tom Frame, *Labouring in Vain: A History of Bishopthorpe*, (Binda, NSW: Saint James, 1996), 65.

unto Thee and he had the feeling that the words of the hymn were not fully considered. He had everybody kneel and sing it again 'thoughtfully' and he invited people to come forward for prayer. The invitation was to just come forward. He assured his congregation that he would not ask any questions but would just pray for them. A number of people came forward to kneel at the communion rail for ministry. No one seemed offended by it and a number felt encouraged.

After the service, a law student asked to see Owen and he invited him to the rectory. "He had read a book by Norman Vincent Peale. He was just reading it on this particular Sunday and he noticed the words, 'If you go to church, expect something to happen to you'. So he made a little pact and he said, 'Very well, I will go to church tonight and I will expect something to happen to me' ... when I had prayed for him, all the depression was lifted off him and he was filled with the Holy Spirit. His whole life turned around really."

This had a profound impact on Owen's ministry. "These days, if I get an urging to do something in my spirit, like a kind of intuition or some sort of urge that comes upon one, I might reject it a few times but if it keeps coming back to me and bugging me, as I know sometimes can happen, I'll follow it." Indeed, he concluded that not everything in ministry was based on logic. There is also a communication in the Spirit. Many years later, the young man attended Owen's consecration to be a bishop at St Andrew's Cathedral in Sydney.

The first Order of St Luke service at St John's was held on Sunday afternoon 17 June 1973. Many more were to follow. In 1979, the first Sunday of the month, at Evensong, there was an opportunity of the ministry of laying on of hands for particular needs. This continued under the next rector of St John's, the Ven. Ian George, former dean of Brisbane.

Owen also encouraged people to make a private confession and seek priestly absolution. In his first Lenten sermons, he preached on the theme of personal renewal. When Owen preached, he preached from the Greek text of the New Testament. And he continued to do this in his ministry.

Owen's musical interests continued at St John's.[25] He led the choir who sang at 11 a.m. and 7.30 p.m. services. But there was a problem with the placement of the organ. The choir sang upstairs in the gallery, but the organ was downstairs in a side porch. Owen wanted to relocate the organ upstairs, but this required a number of structural changes, including strengthening the gallery. The proposed new organ was controversial, leading to a series of parish meetings. The controversy was of such intensity that Owen later commented, "I nearly lost my job". Eventually, Bishop Warren heard the various views, judged in favour of the proposal and granted the faculty for alterations to be made to the church. The cost of the organ was covered by fundraising and the project was completed in the time of the next rector. It was installed and dedicated by Owen as Assistant Bishop on 27 September 1981.

There were lighter moments. Owen was a member of the Metropolitan Lion's Club and he was fined for raising money for the erection of the rector's organ! Apparently, humour abounded.

Owen's son Matthew appreciated his father's wise advice. Matthew was starting to attend parties as a teenager and Owen said, "Don't mix your drinks and avoid people with a bottle in their hand". He also recalled that his father would always listen, was never judgmental and reluctant to give advice. Also, Owen said, "If I was ever to become a Catholic, I'd have to compromise my intellectual integrity". Matthew added, "We thank God for him. We treasure all his gifts and insights that he shared with us all: literature, poetry, music and the life of the Spirit ... where the moth and rust do not corrupt (or in a spoonerism he once made during a *1662 Book of Common Prayer* service: 'where the wrath and must do not corrupt')".

Sheila Thompson was the organist and director of music at St John's for 35 years. She recalled questioning Owen's choice

---

25 Lawrence Bartlett and Owen Dowling, *Music and an Australian Prayer Book*, (Sydney: AIO Press, 1978), 1-24.

of a hymn. Once, never again! She thought it might have been unfamiliar to the congregation. He said with confidence, "Everyone here sings what is put in front of them". He could lead the singing with such strength that the congregation easily followed. On another occasion, when playing a metrical psalm, she included a 'gathering note' and he commented to her, "This is not a Presbyterian Church, we don't have gathering notes".

Owen was active in the wider church. In 1975, he was president of the Canberra Ministers Fraternal. Various members of St Johns helped Owen with work on *The Australian Hymn Book*. His daughter Mary remembered her father working on this over the years and he considered it one of his great achievements in life.

There was considerable life in the parish. Mr Alf Body noted that there was very little cohesion between the five congregations. They met at different times and had distinct styles of worship. Owen made efforts to bridge the gaps. Supper dances and parish picnics were held in 1973 and 1974. The Women's Movement held several progressive diners. In 1975, there were parish dinners aimed at bringing parishioners together. In 1978, the parish had a social gathering associated with the patronal festival. A sense of local mission was not neglected. A Vietnamese refugee family, the Ho family, were welcomed and assisted to settle in Canberra. Various committees from parish council were formed and by 1980 there were committees on mission, visitation and membership growth.[26]

Owen was involved in the community. Matthew began to attend the School Without Walls – a local experiment in education. The staff wanted to provide a more permissive expression of secondary education. Unfortunately, the school became somewhat troubled with some students using drugs and resisting any form of discipline. However, Matthew was self-motivated and became intensely interested in French culture. He went on to study French and eventually received a first-class honours degree from the ANU

---

26 *Firm Still you Stand*, p. 312.

and a DLitt from the Sorbonne in Paris. Owen attended a parent's meeting and was elected chair of School Council.

Owen was developing his media skills. He did regular 30-second spots, along with other Canberra clergy, for the Canberra Christian Television Association. He learned to communicate through this medium and to provide a few simple statements that were easy grabs for the television producer. He continued this through his years of ministry in Canberra. He also participated in religious programs on radio 2CA.

The 1970s were times of significant changes in the Anglican Church. Most of the people at St John's welcomed the new prayer book and hymn book. However, there was some hesitancy about 'sharing the peace' in the service, since this involved shaking hands with fellow worshippers. There was always the option of attending a more traditional older-style services at 7 a.m. and 11 a.m. which did not include the practice. Eventually, sharing the peace became routine.

This was also a time when the congregation got to know the Dowling's dog Vibes – of mixed breed, large and black, never desexed. Sheila Thompson recalled that Vibes would stand beside Owen giving out the Holy Communion and if a parishioner came forward that he did not like, he would growl, though this happened rarely. Clearly, Owen loved animals and Vibes was devoted to him. Vibes died from a broken penis, probably kicked 'in the act'.

Ms Ailsa Curtis, who has been a parishioner for many years, recalled a time when Prince Charles was visiting the church. He asked Owen how long he had been rector. Owen replied, "Eight years". And the prince commented, "Oh, have they forgotten you?" After a much longer wait, Charles is now King Charles III.

At St John's, changes were happening in the Sunday 9:30 a.m. service. The Joy Singers, led by Mr Mark Durie,[27] provided contemporary music. The service became very popular, especially with younger people including university students. The church

---

27 Later, Mark became an academic, with a PhD from ANU in linguistics and was ordained a priest, serving in the Diocese of Melbourne.

was full Sunday after Sunday. On occasion, even larger family services were held in the hall. A Communion in the Round service began with rows of chairs circling the altar. It was informal. Some worshippers would sit on an area of carpet or on cushions. Instead of the traditional preaching, the sermon consisted of discussion around a theme. On occasion, there was a time of ministry. I remember the Communion in the Round services continuing in the years after Owen's ministry. I was a curate and then later Senior Associate Priest after I returned from graduate studies in Boston.

At St John's, Owen developed a Thursday evening fellowship group. This involved a Life in the Spirit course with an emphasis on renewal and the healing ministry, gifts of the spirit, and speaking in tongues. Owen identified with the charismatic renewal. Eventually, he received the gift of speaking in tongues. He recalled, "I had been prayed over for this to happen and absolutely nothing happened to me. I didn't have any heavenly visions or speak in strange languages or whatever. Then, about 12 months later, after I had gone to bed, after some quite exciting spiritual event, I was lying there in bed and suddenly I started to speak in tongues, so one never knows when these gifts might come". This group also continued for some time after Owen left St John's, but as I recall it was not as lively as in Owen's time and soon ended.

Owen was active in the diocese. He led what was called POD, the Parochial Organisation Division, and which examined parish structures, including parishes that were struggling to survive – how they might be restructured along with other parishes and whether ecumenical ministries were appropriate. Owen was next-in-line for assistant bishop, a position occupied by Bishop Neville Chynoweth. Neville was elected to be See of Gippsland. Bishop Warren then let Owen know that that it was his intention to nominate him to the diocesan council.

As I write this, I am impressed with how flexible Bishop Warren was in this appointment. Owen had a very different style in ministry, but the diocesan bishop was able to see his enormous ability and suitability for an episcopal role. He did not hesitate to promote Owen to the episcopal 'boy's club'. It was also clear that after 9 years at St John's, in a high profile ministry in the national capital, Owen was ready to assume a greater role in the church. He was ready 'to fill the mitre' of a bishop.

It is also important to note how innovative Owen was in his pastoral ministry at St Johns. He had the 'Midas touch', everything turned to gold. The people happily supported his various initiatives in musical diversity, liturgical innovation, healing and personal renewal. He led; people followed.

Chapter 8

Life as an Assistant Bishop

The Anglican Diocese of Canberra and Goulburn was first established as the Diocese of Goulburn in 1863, under Letters Patent issued by Queen Victoria. At that time Goulburn became Australia's first inland city. In 1950, the diocese was renamed the Diocese of Canberra and Goulburn, reflecting the growth and development of Canberra as the national capital. The cathedral of the diocese remains St Saviour's Cathedral in Goulburn.

The Diocese of Canberra and Goulburn covers a large area: all of the Australian Capital Territory (ACT), the south-eastern corner of NSW, extending as far as Wagga Wagga in the west (Albury was originally part of the diocese), Marulan in the north and the far South Coast. Each of these regions has a distinctive history and differing senses of community. Ministry is provided to people in rural, regional and city areas. The Diocesan Office is now located in Canberra.[28]

The story now enters a period of transition. Owen had attained some distinction as the rector of St John's Canberra. There was a sense that he could go no further unless he 'wore the purple' of a bishop in the Anglican Church. He was sponsored by the diocesan bishop, the Rt Rev'd Cecil Warren.

There was some risk in accepting the role of an assistant bishop. Owen explained, "You never know whether you are going

---

28 See the excellent diocesan history by Tom Frame, *Church for a Nation: A History of the Anglican Diocese of Canberra and Goulburn*, (Alexandria, NSW, Hale and Ironmonger, 2000).

to be an assistant bishop for life, and it is a little bit hazardous. However, when dioceses are looking around for bishops to elect, they often look at the assistant bishops to see who might appeal to them". Owen was duly consecrated on 25 March 1981, the Feast of the Annunciation of the Blessed Virgin Mary, at St Andrew's Cathedral, Sydney.

He recalled the choir sang an anthem by Samuel Sebastian Wesley called *Thou wilt keep him in Perfect Peace, whose Mind is stayed on Thee* just before hands were laid on him. Owen, while kneeling, opened his eyes. "I decided, in the midst of the prayer, to see what it looked like. It was just like being in a beautiful red tent, because all the 16 bishops that were laying hands on me with Archbishop Loane, they were all wearing red robes, red chimeres, and they were all in a circle around me. When I opened my eyes, they were praying for me and ordaining me. I looked and there was this most beautiful vision of a red tent with light coming in at places all the way round the circle, a most beautiful thing." He also connected his consecration as bishop with his commitment to the Order of St Luke, so he was determined to nod his head in response to the words 'heal the sick'.

Owen was an assistant bishop for two and a half years. This was something of an apprenticeship. He gained experience and learnt from Bishop Warren. As always, such learning was a 'mixed bag' and included both positive and negative aspects of episcopal ministry. Owen recognised the strengths of his diocesan bishop. "He was a very systematic kind of person, well organised and thoughtful and a real gentleman. Cecil – there was no doubt about it – and a very competent bishop ... he had wide experience. He had travelled quite a bit and he introduced some good things into Canberra and Goulburn. Every time he went away on a trip he would try to go and learn something which would be helpful to the diocese here rather than to just have a holiday."

Cursillo is an example. This is a renewal movement which he brought to Australia from Canada. It caught on and soon spread to other dioceses and denominations. Cursillo is called the Emmaus Walk in the Uniting Church.

Owen recalled taking his first service as a bishop. "The first Sunday I went out as a bishop into the diocese, I went to Crookwell. Being new, holding my shepherd's crook, my pastoral staff, which [Mr] John Watch, a friend, had kindly made for me, [he] steamed and bent the wood so I had this nice, simple, pastoral staff, a shepherd's crook, which doesn't get broken every time it falls over as some staffs do ... So as I was holding this thing, I thought I had better say something about it. I said to the congregation there at Crookwell, 'I don't think they use these things anymore, but you know what they are for. They are really for caring for the sheep' and I talked about the symbolism of it."

When Owen became an assistant bishop, Beverly refused to wash his purple shirts, since they needed to be washed by hand. It was a task that Owen accepted.

Owen took the opportunity to do further study. He joined a collegium of senior clergy doing a Doctor of Ministry (DMin) degree offered by the Presbyterian San Francisco Theological Seminary. The Uniting Church in Australia encouraged their clergy to treat the DMin as advanced education for experienced clergy. A group of graduate students met for an afternoon every fortnight, occasionally for a whole day or a weekend. It was an opportunity to reflect on ministry, as Owen said, "I found this all intensely interesting and helpful, especially as I was getting launched into being a bishop. I had to reflect on the nature of Episcopal ministry and the nature of the changes that were taking place in my life". He also attended a summer school in 1982 at San Anselmo, a suburb of San Francisco. Later, Owen regretted not being able to finish his dissertation due to the demands of becoming a diocesan bishop.

Bishop Warren nominally divided the diocese into two halves. Each year, he would alternate the responsibility for an area with his assistant bishop. Owen also focused on the pastoral and spiritual aspects of life in the diocese. He formed a retreat committee, which encouraged clergy and lay people to take an opportunity for personal renewal. The renovated Bishopthorpe became a centre of spirituality in the diocese. Owen's children recalled their parents having close couple friends including the Rev'd Colin and Ms Dorothy Tunbridge, Professor Adrian and Ms Audrey Horridge, Professor Bob and Ms Helen Crompton, and the Rev'd John and Ms Barbara Griffiths. There was a revolving cycle of meals together.

After 18 months as an assistant bishop, Owen was approached to be the Bishop of Tasmania. However, he did not allow his name to go forward to the electoral synod because he needed more time in the assistant role. In his last year as assistant bishop, Owen assumed the role of Acting Principal of the College of Ministry, where he had some influence on students training for the priesthood.

It was natural for Owen to want to take the next step and serve as a diocesan bishop. But he was willing to be patient and await the right time – even in the face of obvious risks. He was also able to put the needs of the Diocese of Canberra and Goulburn before his own self-interest, and not jump at the first opportunity of a see.

Chapter 9

Elected Bishop of Canberra and Goulburn

The Diocese of Canberra and Goulburn has been fortunate in the service of many fine diocesan bishops. The following is a brief sketch of those, prior to Bishop Owen. The first was the Rt Rev'd Mesac Thomas (1816–1892). He was consecrated in Canterbury Cathedral and appointed to the Diocese of Goulburn in 1863, He arrived in Australia a year later. The cathedral was completed in his time and Bishopthorpe was built as a home for bishops in the diocese. He was an evangelical who died in office and was buried at his cathedral.

The next bishop was the Rt Rev'd William Chalmers (1833–1901). He had previously been a missionary serving the Dyak people in Borneo. He was one of the founders of the Australian College of Theology and he served as bishop for nine years (1892–1901). Chalmers achieved a settlement in the long running 'cathedral dispute'[29] and was highly regarded as a pastor who helped the diocese towards a more broad and inclusive churchmanship.[30]

The Rt Rev'd Christopher Barlow (1858–1915) came from the Diocese of North Queensland to become the third bishop of the diocese. He was the first Australian ordained priest to become a bishop.[31] He served the diocese from 1902–1915. He

---

29 Bill Wright, *Shepherds in a New Country: Bishops in the Diocese of Canberra and Goulburn 1837-1993*, (Self-published, 1993), 10.
30 Frame, *Church for a Nation*, 98.
31 Wright, *Shepherds in a New Country*, 12.

established a short-lived theological college, the Clergy Training College, Goulburn, in 1906. In 1908, he brought a car back from England and was the first bishop to have motorised transport in Australia. The diocese continued to grow both in the number of parishes and ordained clergy.

The Rt Rev'd Dr Lewis Radford (1869-1937), a graduate of Cambridge and an academic at St Paul's College University of Sydney, became the next bishop serving from 1915-1933. The Churchwomen's Union began in 1916 and was nurtured by his wife. The two grammar schools in Canberra owe a lot to his foresight. The Community of the Ascension was established in 1921 at Bishopthorpe, the first Anglican male monastic order established in Australia. Radford was elitist in his attitudes[32] but sympathetic to Anglo-Catholic practice. He promoted the role of the Anglican church in the national capital and in 1926 proposed a national cathedral to General Synod (without success, but the diocese gained the St Mark's site).[33]

The longest serving bishop in the diocese was the Rt Rev'd Ernest Burgmann (1885-1967) who was diocesan bishop from 1934 to 1960. He had a rural background, leaving school at 14, becoming expert in skills involving horses, wielding an axe, bullock team driving and shooting. He gained his LTh doing part-time study but later went to Sydney University to graduate with both BA and MA. He gained a reputation for scholarship, writing a number of books and articles. He established a training college on the St Mark's site. The Young Anglican Movement was formed in 1938. Bergmann pursued issues of social justice and his ideas on environmental matters were prophetic.[34]

In 1946, he moved the bishop's residence to Canberra and the diocese was renamed Canberra and Goulburn in 1950. In 1954, Queen Elizabeth II, the first reigning British monarch to visit

---

32 Frame, *Church for a Nation*, 123.
33 See Paul Radford, *A Scholar in a New Land: A Biography of Lewis Bostock Radford*, (South Australia: Flinders University, 1979).
34 Wright, *Shepherds...*, p. 16.

Australia, worshipped with the people of the diocese. St Mark's Anglican National Memorial Library opened in 1957 and Bishop Burgmann served as warden until 1964.[35]

The Rt Rev'd Kenneth Clements (1905-1992) served as diocesan bishop from 1961–1971. He studied at Sydney University and trained at St John's, Morpeth. He became the first coadjutor (assistant) bishop in the diocese under Bergmann. He was elected to Grafton Diocese and returned to Canberra and Goulburn in 1961. His years were marked by the rapid expansion of Canberra and the establishing of parishes in new suburbs. Soon after he arrived, the diocese celebrated its centenary with the *Forward in Faith* program lead by his successor. In 1966, the Diocesan Development Fund was established. Jamieson House was opened and accommodated the diocesan registry.

The Rt Rev'd Cecil Warren (1924-2019) became the 7th bishop of the diocese and served 1972-1983. He was educated at the University of Sydney (BA) and Oxford (MA). He also tried unsuccessfully to persuade the national Anglican church to take up the cause of the Anglican national cathedral proposed by Radford.[36] For 17 years, he was chairperson of the production committee of *An Australian Prayer Book* published in 1978. He introduced the Cursillo movement to the diocese in 1979. I remember Cecil as a generous and fair-minded man. He was socially awkward, but astute in his judgment of people. He was not especially pastoral.[37]

Bishop Warren had been the Bishop of Canberra and Goulburn for 12 years. He decided 'to retire' to be an assistant bishop and rector of a parish in Derby, England. This left the role of diocesan

---

35 A comprehensive biography is Peter Hemenstall, *The Meddlesome Priest: A Life of Ernest Burgmann*, (St Leonards, NSW: Allen and Unwin,1993).

36 This project effectively ended in 1986 when the government refused to give the project tax deductibility status, so it went on "freeze". Synod address 1986.

37 See his autobiography, C. A. Warren, *A Little Foolishness: An Autobiographical History*, (Virginia QLD: Church Archival Press, 1993). There is little mention of Bishop Owen.

bishop open. Numerous contenders came forward, including the Rev'd Dr David Penman, who later became the Archbishop of Melbourne, the Rt Rev'd Oliver Hayward, the Bishop of Bendigo, and the Rev'd Canon Peter Hollingworth, later Archbishop of Brisbane, Primate and Governor General of Australia. Clearly, Owen had significant competition.

The election synod went ahead in 1983. Initially, Owen was involved in the process. "I remember the experience of it quite well. I was the president of the Synod, being the administrator of the diocese, so I had to summon the Synod and celebrate the opening Eucharist and then be in the Synod. Then, when the nominations were read out, I had to absent myself from the Synod, my name being one of them. Beverly and I went up to Bishopthorpe and we spent the day there on a Saturday." In his absence, about 300 delegates debated the merits of the various candidates.

Owen had been informed that he was one of the last two 'in the race'. The election process took all Saturday with initial nominations first cut to four, and then to two with the final election happening after a dinner break. One participant recalled the evening session being highly emotional. I had heard that the Rev'd David Durie had appealed to Synod, "We just need someone to love us!" Owen was called back without knowing whether he had been elected. The chancellor Mr Jim Munro said, "I have pleasure in announcing that you have been elected as the bishop of the diocese". Owen was then greeted with applause. For the record, he was elected 15 November 1983.

Warren and Dowling were very different bishops. Cecil was the kind of leader needed for a growing diocese. He was a good administrator and highly strategic in his thinking. But no one could describe him as personable. Owen was the complete opposite: warm, engaging and genuinely interested in everyone around him. Another great strength that Owen brought to his new role was his capacity to unite the Evangelical, liberal and charismatic elements of the church. Ms Lynlea Rodger noted that his Christianity was broad enough, that each group could relax in a 'space for mutual connection'.

In the minutes of Bishop-in-Council, there is an interesting note that Archdeacon Ian George proposed the Bishop of Canberra and Goulburn be named as an Archbishop. However, a few months later, the Standing Committee of General Synod declined, and the minutes also noted that the Bishops' Conference was also negative.[38] Eventually, Ian would become an Archbishop (of Adelaide), but Owen did not.

A month later, Owen was installed in St Saviours Cathedral, Goulburn.[39] He enjoyed a wide measure of support in the diocese. On a more personal note, he reflected, "There is always that talk about 'special favourites' and all that sort of thing, which you have to try and guard against as a bishop. I can remember one friend of mine who was a junior clergy person in the diocese, decided to move on because people thought of him as one of my 'favourites'. He happened to be a good friend of mine". He was describing his friendship with the Very Rev'd Peter Williams, now a senior Roman Catholic priest. Peter is a fine musician and he met Owen when he was a university student at ANU. Peter became a very close friend of Owen, Beverly and the children. On a number of occasions, he went on holidays with the Dowling's and was considered a member of the family. Peter observed that Owen "deeply loved" his wife. He remembered Owen as very transparent. He was not frightened to disclose if he was going through an anxious time. He would also share your burdens and engage in a wide range of conversation.

After Owen was installed as diocesan bishop, he began to sign the minutes of Bishop-in-Council +Owen Canberra and Goulburn. He was struck by the formalities of his new office, "One was the first time that I had to sign a document after I had been installed as the Bishop of Canberra and Goulburn. It said, 'We, Owen Douglas, by divine providence or permission, Lord Bishop of Canberra and Goulburn do, by these presence...' et cetera, et cetera. It was a legal and formal document. It rather shocked me

---

38 Pages 41 and 65.
39 17 December 1983.

when I had to sign my name to a document which started 'We'." Owen consulted with the chancellor and when possible changed documents to 'I, Owen Douglas ...' He also made some minor liturgical changes such as the Bishop's chaplain walking in front of the bishop during a procession.

Owen also made the appointment process of clergy to parishes more consultative. The Clergy Presentation Board was made up of three representatives from the diocese and the same number from the parish. Only the Bishop could present a formal nomination to the board, who could only say yes or no. If three nominations were rejected, then the bishop could appoint without further consultation. Owen valued an open discussion about possibilities. He also encouraged suggestions from the committee. Only then would Owen make a formal nomination. He also saw some benefit in interviews with candidate priests.

There were many advantages to such an open and collaborative process. For example, the parish representatives were more likely to feel that they 'owned' the decision. Owen also invited clergy in the diocese, if they had been in a position for at least three years, to tell him if they were interested in a move to a new parish. He observed something that I have noticed as well. "It is a funny dynamic in the church of people being quite ambitious but not liking to admit that they are ambitious for a particular job and then feeling very disgruntled if not considered."

There was an amusing incident in July 1984 when Owen was dedicating Holy Covenant Church, Jamieson. When he, as part of the liturgy, knocked three times with his pastoral staff on the door of the church and called all out, "May I enter?" From inside the building, Sam Gilmour, a young child, said, "No! No! Not by the hair of my chinney, chin, chin. I'll not let you in!"[40]

Owen had a relational style of leadership. He would see Diocesan ordination candidates, while students, three times a year. He met with archdeacons and senior clergy before Bishop

---

40 Beverly Barnes, *A Noble Experiment: A History of Holy Covenant Anglican parish*, 1992, p. 75.

in Council meetings, to discuss pending issues. He established a one-day clergy conference to discuss the year ahead. In Holy Week, he led a clergy quiet day with a renewal of ordination vows in the cathedral. There was an opportunity for prayer ministry at this time; indeed, Owen encouraged his clergy to pray for one another.

I vaguely recall being on a diocesan clergy retreat with Owen as the leader. It is sometimes useful to practise the discipline of confession and I went to him as my 'father in God'. I have no memory of what I confessed, but I would recall if I had not been absolved! He was more to me than the CEO of the diocese.

Owen kept up his sporting interests. This included playing squash with the Rev'd Andrew Knight. Andrew recalled that he was 26 years old at the time, more fit, but Owen was so good at placing the ball on the court that Andrew never won a game! Perhaps this also indicates how competitive Owen could be.[41] The Rev'd Keith McCollim also played squash with Owen, but managed to hold his own. Keith recalled Owen saying about the attractive parish of Narooma, on the south coast and near the beach, "Why has God told 12 of my clergy that they were to apply?"

Owen encouraged outreach by having parish missions. Usually, this would involve an evangelistic outreach, with a parish singing group, and having a gathering in the street or at the shopping centre. He would typically include a healing service. Often, the parish would be encouraged to have a dinner in a local club and invite civic leaders. He would speak to them about the Christian faith and about the church's vision.

He did a number of missions around Australia and repeatedly went to PNG (four times). He remembered, "An open-air meeting in Port Moresby, a woman came staggering out of hospital, who had extremely far advanced cancer. She came forward for prayer and she was completely healed". This was confirmed when he saw her again a year later when she was completely clear of cancer. He

---

41 After the scandal, there was some comment among clergy about him playing squash with Owen, but Andrew said, "There was never a hint of anything [inappropriate] with me".

said, "I developed quite a bit of experience being up front and speaking more or less off the cuff; being able to speak directly to people, not only speak to them but I used to sing to them also. I remember that there is a song called *Tell my people I love them, Tell my people I care*, which is a song I used to use quite a bit."

He ministered to the wider church and held missions in South Templestowe in Melbourne; then at Horsham in Victoria; Castlemaine; Broken Hill; Endeavour Hills in Melbourne; and Hornsby in Sydney. He also went to Nungalinya College, which is the ecumenical college in Darwin for training Aboriginal people for ministry. He returned to PNG. "In 1986, I went with Dan Armstrong, who was then the minister of the O'Connor Uniting Church. We were invited by the ministers' fraternal in Port Moresby to do a mission. The plan was that I would attend to the healing aspect of the teaching and the ministry and Dan Armstrong would concentrate on the evangelism. In one meeting, in a country area, about two thousand people responded as a group to the invitation to believe in Christ."

Owen thought that such a corporate decision was no less valid than an individual one. His enthusiasm for missions was an expression of what I had observed about Owen: he enjoyed ministry, bringing the resources of God, to individuals and building up the body of Christ.

Once, he was momentarily without words, given the cross-cultural setting and need for an interpreter, but a breeze came through. "Then I said, 'Well, we believe that the wind of the Spirit is coming to revive us and renew us and help us to do the things of God'. So I spoke then about Pentecost and the coming of the Spirit at Pentecost and the fact that not only had Peter and the other apostles preached the gospel, but they immediately also began a healing ministry." There were long lines of people and many were miraculously healed. When Owen returned to PNG, he took a small team of people from the diocese to help him. He considered such missions to be 'front line work'.[42]

Owen was very effective in parish missions. When I was doing graduate studies in Boston, I was the part-time rector of St Paul's, Millis. Owen came to visit and carried out a mission in 1986 which was well received by the congregation. I also remember a funny incident when he stayed with us. Jennie and I vacated our double bed to offer Owen the main bedroom. We were sleeping below in the cellar. Owen was on our 'op shop' bed which had seen better days. With some regularity it would collapse, and it did this with Owen and about 2 a.m. in the morning. We heard a crash above us!

Owen changed the name of the annual appeal from the Bishop's Poverty Appeal to the Bishop's Welfare Appeal, and it eventually became Care Force with a strong contribution to various needs in the diocese. This included ministry to children, youth and the aged. He also worked to build up the Diocesan Foundation which supported ministry in the diocese. Owen attempted to bridge the country/city divide and used a video made by Mr Rob Warren-Smith, a media consultant. In the Synod of 1986, there was a proposal to coordinate the welfare programs of the church, which Owen described as intending to give "a more definite structure and intentionality to our work".[43]

Owen was involved in practical aspects of diocesan administration. He set up the Buildings and Faculties Committee. They reviewed building plans and petitions for faculties, for any changes in buildings, such as the introduction of artworks and ornaments into the church, can only be done after a faculty has been granted. The committee was coordinated by the registrar, had an architect, a builder, a clergy wife and several other knowledgeable people. Owen would wait for proposals to be assessed by the committee before giving his permission for a change to be made.

Owen appointed two assistant bishops in his time, both from within the diocese. The first was Bishop Bruce Wilson consecrated

---

42 Synod address 1986, 5.
43 Synod address 1986, 12.

27 October 1984. He was later elected bishop of Bathurst. Then Archdeacon Ian George was consecrated 28 October 1989. Later he became Archbishop of Adelaide in 1991. Both were made bishop in St Saviour's Cathedral, Goulburn, which was a change from the tradition of using the cathedral in Sydney.[44]

In his time as Bishop, Owen was involved in a gathering of Christians to mark the beginning of the parliamentary year. This occasion was organised by Fusion and offered an opportunity to remember the Myall Creek massacre of indigenous people. In the incident mainly women and children were herded into a cattle coral and slaughtered. In talking to local Aboriginal people, it was found that they still had some of the timbers from the Myall Creek cattle yard. A cross was made. Some of the church leaders, both from Aboriginal and mainstream churches, took it in turns to carry the cross on their shoulder. Owen had the experience, "[As] I was walking along with it, as I had the timber right against my ear, I could hear the cries of the people who were slaughtered in that corral. Now this may be fanciful of course... But I have a very strong conviction that the wood of that timber still contained the agony and the rejection and the pain and the cries of the people who had been slaughtered there and, of course the whole tradition of hurt that Aboriginal people have suffered".

Owen was to face a great loss. His wife Beverly was found to have breast cancer. "She had an operation, a lumpectomy, on her breast on 11th October 1984. I remember that because it was my 50th birthday. We were having a family dinner that night and we were getting the result from the doctor. He told me on the phone then that it was pretty bad ... So I knew that night that there was every possibility that she would die." They tried radiotherapy and, when the cancer returned, chemotherapy, but she contracted pneumonia and this probably contributed to her death. In this "gruesome time", he recalled, "at the end of the dinner [which Owen had prepared] she was sitting by the fire. It was a winter's

---

44 Bill Wright, *Shepherds in a New Country: Bishops in the Diocese of Canberra and Goulburn 1837-1993*, (Self published booklet 1993), 24.

night and she was due to go back to the hospital on the Sunday evening. She said to me, 'I can go now'. I said, 'Oh yes. Yes, I'll take you soon. We must go back to the hospital'. She said, 'No, I didn't mean that'. She said, 'I think it's okay for me to die because I can see that you can manage'. She said, 'You can put on a good dinner like this and you will be able to cope and I can see that so I feel I can go'. I was quite moved by that". She also gave Owen her permission to marry again after her death. He added, "I think I was prepared to release her too by the time she died".

The children remembered a somewhat ironic incident. On the day that Beverly received the news that cancer has spread to her liver, Owen picked up Lamb's fry from the butcher for the evening meal. When Matthew said something to him about being insensitive, Owen's response was, "It was on special". Beverly laughed. The Dowling family life was often full of laughter with a sense of humour coming to the fore in difficult times.

A week or so before Beverly died in 1985, she had a comforting dream. She was on a train with all sorts of people including some she knew and some she didn't. The train was going to Samarkand. She had a sense of going somewhere and life beyond the grave.

Bishop Bruce Wilson cared for the family as Beverly deteriorated. At her death bed, Owen recalled, "Matthew, one of my sons, who always has quite a good instinct about what to do. He started to speak to Beverly even though she was there lying unconscious. I recognised the fact that seemingly unconscious people can hear. He started telling Beverly all that she had meant to him and how precious she was to him. Then each of us, in our turn, talked to her".

The next day, in the middle of the day, she opened her eyes when Tim, their oldest, was sitting by the bed, and she said, 'I'm here'. She only said those two words. Later, as she was dying, she had a wailing fit, which Owen could hardly bear to hear but a nurse said, 'No, stay'. He was glad that he did.

In his 1985 Synod address, Owen gave tribute to Beverly, "She was a model of confidentiality. Many would open their hearts to her because they sensed some of her own pain and struggles ... I never heard her gossip or pass on anything of a confidential nature.

Rather, I felt a foot pressing against mine on occasions and I knew that she thought I was saying too much."

The Archbishop of Canterbury, Robert Runcie, visited the diocese in April 1985 and again to bless the cathedral bells in March 1987. The cathedral tower was commenced in 1986 as an Australian Bicentennial project and dedicated on Advent Sunday, 27 November 1988. On 4 May 1986, the Albury parishes were transferred to the Diocese of Wangaratta.

Owen was chair of the Liturgical Commission for the Anglican Church in Australia. At this time, a number of new experimental services were published. The commission was working towards the revision of the *Australian Prayer Book* (1978) which was published in 1995. The Rev'd Gill Varcoe was an editor and recalled that the commission worked well together. The committee responded to Owen's leadership.

Owen with a priest in the diocese of Canberra and Goulburn

Owen engaged the wider church as the author of the 1989 Lenten study book *Power to be Witnesses*.[45] And he was the warden of the Order of Saint Luke in Australia from 1987 to 1992.

The 1985 General Synod was concerned about the role of the primacy. What was to be the relationship of the Bishop and his [at that time his] diocese if such primacy was to be located in Canberra? It was decided to launch another appeal for the National Anglican Centre on the St Mark's site, but again this failed because the national church did not have the resolve or the resources.[46] Owen was on the Canberra planning committee for the Seventh Assembly of the World Council of Churches and attended as a guest in 1991.

Owen was also a supporter of ARMA (Anglican Renewal Ministries Australia). He was widely known as a charismatic bishop. But he took it lightly. The Ven. Des McGuire recalled talking to Owen, just before he became Rector of Chapman. Des asked whether Owen thought the Holy Spirit was in the appointment? Owen, with a twinkle in his eye, replied, "I am not sure the Spirit gets through when we are appointing clergy, but he corrects our mistakes".

Owen suffered a mild heart attack in December 1989 and had triple bypass surgery a month later. He was on leave for seven months. Later, he took some months sick leave in 1992.[47] In that year, he attended the funerals of two bishops: his predecessor Kenneth Clements and Gordon Arthur.[48]

---

45 Owen Dowling, *Power to be Witnesses*, (Sydney: Anglican Information Office, 1988). ISBN 978-0-949108-81-4. There are 49 daily studies reflecting on passages from the Book of Acts and participants were encouraged to meet weekly through Lent to discuss suggested themes.
46 Bill Wright, *Shepherds in a New Country*, 25.
47 Wright, *Shepherds in a New Country*, 25.
48 Owen spoke at the National Press Club, Canberra, 12 February 1992, Trove has an audio recording.

One of Owen's great strengths was his availability. The Rev'd Robin Miners was appointed to the parish of St Mary in the Valley and Owen acknowledged this as "a leading of the Holy Spirit which couldn't be denied". Later, a freak 'willi-willi' [tornado] destroyed their church building. Just after Owen's surgery, he attended incognito and supported Robin and lay leaders. Robin also recalled a previous occasion he was asked – when still a student at St Mark's – to drive Owen to do a funeral for a clergy wife in Junee and then dedicate a church in Wagga Wagga and return to Canberra – all in one day!

Peter Williams remembered the only argument that he had with Owen. It was when he refused the offer of the parish of Queanbeyan, which he felt was too tied to the ministry of the previous rector. In the heat of the argument, Owen shouted at him. In part, Owen thought it was arranged, but possibly it was because he wanted to keep his friend close to Canberra. A few weeks later, Peter accepted a parish in the Diocese of Wangaratta. A few years later, Peter became a Roman Catholic priest. Owen attended the ceremony at the Parramatta Cathedral, but Peter didn't think that he fully understood the reasons he left the Anglican Church. He accepted it "because it was me".[49]

In 1985, General Synod began to seriously consider the ordination of women in the Anglican Church. Years before, Owen had been asked to take part in a debate on this topic at a clergy conference. He was assigned the negative side – to say no. He won popular support but had a negative reaction. "I realised this wasn't a game and I had used some arguments that I didn't know whether I really believed in. I thought I had been a bit unfair too. I had probably disparaged women and their role in the church and in society and their gifts and I felt really bad about it. It made me rethink the thing."

---

49 One Christmas when Peter was rector of Yea, all the Dowling family – Owen, Beverley and the children – travelled to Victoria to spend Christmas with him.

Owen attended his first General Synod in 1973 and the ordination of women to the diaconate was being debated. It was decided not to recognise a deaconess as a deacon. Owen thought this was a poor decision. He could not agree with the argument that Christ was male, therefore priests should be male. He thought the main point was that Christ was human and having women ordained is part of that fullness of humanity. In 1985, the canon was finally passed to admit women to the diaconate.

However, there were three failed attempts at the General Synods of 1985, 1987 and 1989 to have women admitted to the priesthood. Motions would pass through the houses of laity and Bishops but narrowly fail to achieve the necessary 2/3rd majority in the house of clergy. Owen was active 'behind the scenes'. He chaired a standing committee of General Synod, which was trying to find ways to get past the deadlock. The synod of Canberra and Goulburn had also expressed support.[50]

Dr Janet Scarfe recalled that, in 1992, Owen Dowling was one of six bishops and archbishops who announced late in 1991 they would ordain women priests. Their announcements were vague about whether they would wait for General Synod's approval but two announced definite dates – Owen Dowling and (later in January) Archbishop Peter Carnley.[51]

It was a time of increasing tension. Owen reflected, "It led up to a climax as we kept being frustrated and could not move. Of course, the women, by this time, some of them had been deacons for several years and some of them had been appointed to parishes. It was already clear that pastorally speaking, and from the point of

---

50 For a history of the process leading to the ordination of women to the priesthood, see Keith Mason's chapter, "Challenging Church Law 'Phillimore's rule', Eds Elaine Lindsay and Janet Scarfe, *Preachers, Prophets and Heretics: Anglican Women's Ministry*, (Sydney: New South Publishing, 2012), 77-94.
51 Janet Scarfe: email 19 January 2023.

view of leadership, there was nothing lacking in the ministry which the women were giving".[52]

After Archbishop David Penman died in 1989, the leadership of the pro-group fell on Owen. He gathered the bishops in favour of the ordination of women and their legal representatives for a meeting to consider what could be done. In 1989, the synod of Canberra and Goulburn passed an ordinance to support the ordination of women should it be legally possible. At this point the Solicitor-General of NSW, Keith Mason QC, expressed the view that it was not necessary to have a canon of the General Synod. There was nothing in the constitution of the Anglican Church of Australia that prevented the ordaining of women.

Owen was convinced. "My argument was that change comes unevenly in the church and then it is regulated after a time. Once change begins to happen, then the church considers it and says, 'Well shall we make this a normal part of the kind of rule, or canons, of the church'?" He also believed that the Holy Spirit led the church in making changes (cf. Acts 15). He decided to act. "It was agreed that I would go ahead as a kind of 'guinea pig' I suppose, that I would stick my neck out."

In his 1990 address to synod, Owen announced he was going to ordain women without a canon from General Synod. He would wait for questions to be answered by the Appellate Tribunal, but then he would proceed. The Tribunal responded in late in 1991. But there was no answer on the crucial legal question. Not a clear yes or no! So Owen made plans to ordain the women deacons as priests along with the men, at the ordination service 2 February 1992.[53] It was a significant event and people came from interstate and overseas.

---

[52] The Rev'd Margaret Streatfield had been appointed as deacon-in-charge of Koorawatha.
[53] The primate, Archbishop Keith Rayner, had asked that no precipitate action be taken to ordain women and that General Synod be given a final chance at its 1992 meeting. Preachers..., 158. There was considerable resistance, the Metropolitan Archbishop Robinson of Sydney instructed Owen to desist but he declined. Also note that Owen's mother Winifred, died on 8 February 1992.

However, an application for an injunction was made. "I was taken to court in January[54] and we were there before Mr Justice Andrew Rogers, who was normally an industrial or commercial judge. He was quite sympathetic to us and our cause." The injunction was not granted, but the case went to the appeal court.[55] Owen sat in the appeal case but had to return for the preordination retreat with a few men and 12 women waiting to be ordained.

The door was shut in their face. Ken Mason rang Owen at Bishopthorpe, in Goulburn. Everyone was on retreat, sitting down to lunch, and awaiting the decision. Owen had the unhappy task of going back into the dining room and saying, "I'm sorry to say that the answer is no". The Rev'd Anne Dudzinski recalled him saying "It is lost!" She also remembered that many of the women, hoping to be priests, had unpicked their deacon stoles so it could hang freely as priests. Their disappointment was profound, and a number began to weep. It was a very dramatic moment. The ABC sent a helicopter and a number of the women were interviewed for the 7.30 Report.[56]

The Rev'd Elaine Gifford, one of the 11, remembered that there was a lot of pressure on Owen to avoid the NSW injunction by moving the ordination to the ACT. But "he was determined to do it the right way", she added. It was significant that the Rev'd Alison Cheek was present at the retreat to support the women. She was one of the eleven women ordained to the priesthood in the USA in 1975 by a retired bishop in an 'irregular' ceremony.

There was an acknowledgment of the women in the service. One of the women candidates, the Rev'd Gill Mendham (now Varcoe), suggested that the women answer the first ordination question in the service: Do you think that you be truly called, according to the will of our Lord Jesus Christ and the order of

---

54 In what was to be called Scandrett v Dowling (1992) 27 NSWLR 483.
55 Chief Justice Gleeson, Justices Samuels and Meagher.
56 The whole program of the 7.30 Report was given to the cancelled ordination.

this Anglican Church of Australia, to the office and order of priesthood? They would answer 'I do'.[57]

It was a public affirmation that that they thought they were called, and then step back. Owen agreed but suggested that the women might then sit down, but Gill insisted that they remain standing. Then the ordination of the men would then proceed. It gave an opportunity for the congregation of the cathedral and those gathered – along with the Bishop – to say that they were truly called, even though there was a court order to forbid it. When it came to the service, voices along the row of candidates were heard, a mixture of high and low, saying, 'I do. I do. I do. I do'. About six along, when it was the Rev Julie Kelly's turn, she shouted out, 'I have absolutely no doubt whatsoever'. At that point, the gathering erupted. People cheered and stamped and shouted.

Gill Varcoe also recalled an incident that happened at the retreat. When she saw the Bishop for a private interview, knowing that her ordination would not proceed, she expressed reservations about taking Holy Communion. "If this is the way the church treats me!" Owen had a sharp reaction. He was furious and shouted at her with the threat that he would not license her. While this must be seen within the context of the 'pressure cooker' retreat, it also says something about the importance Owen placed on Holy Communion in the life of the church. Gill remembered her ordination vow of promising to obey her Bishop, and, on the day, she received Communion.

Dr Scarfe recalled the service as 'absolutely harrowing' and argued that it should never have taken the form of ordaining only the men while the women stood, watched and wept. She thought Owen should have defied the injunction. She acknowledged that some would argue his act was a powerful statement that actually increased support for women's ordination. But Janet made the valid point that, if this was the case, it was an extraordinarily cruel

---

57 She had been a deacon for five years and when she attended ordination services it was her practice to say a quiet, "I do", in anticipation of one day being admitted to the priesthood.

way of making the point. Seeing some of the men undeniably happy at their own priesting made it worse although the service has gone down in history as the 'non-ordination'.

A number of the men were reluctant to proceed, in sympathy with the women, but all were ordained on the day. Janet remains somewhat cynical about the sincerity of the commitment by church leaders to women's ministry, and their understanding of the cost to women, as that day symbolised. Elaine Gifford recalled that, because it was a significant step for her to reach that point, it was a big step and, so it was a big letdown when the ordination was denied. Gill Varcoe had a different reaction. She saw that the legal injunction would backfire on the opponents. "I knew that day that we had won."

Geoff Prior, *Canberra Times*, used with permission

The injunction then went to a full hearing of the court. This was a few months later and the court decided not to interfere in ecclesiastical matters. The way was now open. Archbishop Peter Carnley of Perth ordained the first group of women to the priesthood (7 March 1992). Owen then felt able to proceed with the ordinance of the 11 women deacons to the priesthood.[58] It was to be one of his final acts as diocesan bishop since he had already announced his resignation. In 1995, General Synod passed the canon allowing the ordination of women.

Owen with Women in Bishopthorpe chapel

Now, 25 years later, we can look back on these dramatic events. By the end of 1992, a total of 99 women had been made priests in the Anglican Church in Australia. The role of women as priests and bishops is now well established. It is normal to have female clergy

---

58 In Bishop-in-Council minutes, there was a motion to set up a fund for the ordination of women to meet legal costs. Elaine Gifford remembered receiving $100, when the fund was not needed for that purpose, as did the other women.

except in a handful of dioceses, under the influence of the Diocese of Sydney. The 'sky did not fall in'.

As an afterthought, I will record Anne Dudzinski's memory of a committee meeting of the Movement for the Ordination of Women at Jamieson House (Registry of the diocese). Owen offered to make the women present a cup of tea – and he did!

How do we evaluate Owen's time as the bishop of Canberra and Goulburn? It was a time of upheaval in the church, but he gave the diocese strong leadership in a direction most of the church would eventually follow. Most significantly, he was a powerful advocate of women's ordination to the priesthood and almost achieved the break-through in the cathedral at Goulburn. But this was not his only contribution to the diocese and wider church – as his record clearly demonstrates. Perhaps Owen had a few weaknesses as a bishop. He was not particularly strategic. He was a spiritual person with a strong focus on pastoral ministry. This is obvious in reading the successive Synod charges he made as diocesan Bishop. He led the way in a cathedral restoration appeal by giving $1000 and inviting 499 other donors to follow to complete the work. But it is hard to find any other significant initiatives in his time.

Over the years, when the rural properties were returning large surpluses, Owen resisted suggestions to think carefully about how to spend the unexpected windfall. His reaction was to fund additional ministry. He did not seem to appreciate the wisdom of Joseph who interpreted Pharaoh's dream of seven fat cows and seven lean cows (Genesis 41:1-36). Perhaps, as Mr Clive Rodger suggested, Owen found it easier to be 'Spirit led' than to plan-ahead.

Bishop George Browning, his successor as diocesan bishop, discovered after six months in the job, that the diocesan foundations and trusts had been borrowed against – effectively emptied. I now understand that Bishop Cecil Warren borrowed against the trust funds to fund the expansion of parishes into new areas of development in Canberra. Bishop George had the task of rebuilding the diocesan reserves, which he did, at least partially through the sale of rural properties.

It could also be said that Bishop Owen was similar to almost every other bishop in the Anglican and Roman Catholic churches in that he was not especially vigilant to the risk of clergy sexually abusing children. There were no accepted guidelines and perhaps he saw his relationship to his clergy as a 'forgiving father in God'. At that time, many diocesan bishops would accept an offenders' 'repentance', believing it to be genuine and their promise not to re-offend. Additionally, perhaps Owen did not want to know. I was told about a priest who went to see Owen to admit to having an affair, but Owen refused to listen. "I don't want to know."

On record are some sad cases of the sexual assault of children in the diocese. John Aitchison, a priest, has been convicted and jailed for offences.[59] A number of people told me that Owen had some awareness of the risks involved with Aitchison, but he did nothing. Keith McCollim, after supervising his unit of Clinical Pastoral Education, had expressed reservations about John's suitability for ministry. Bishop Jeff Driver noted that church leaders of the time had little understanding of grooming and some paedophiles invested considerable time and energy grooming bishops and other leaders in the church. Another priest, Taffy Cole, was moved to Junee after offending with members of the youth group and eventually ended up in jail. I am pleased that the church appears to have learnt something of a lesson in recent years.[60]

Tom Frame published a history of the Diocese of Canberra and Goulburn (on the 50th anniversary of its renaming).[61] He observed that Bishop Owen was similar in outlook to the pastoral bishops

---

59 The Aitchison case was featured in an article in the Canberra Times Sunday, February 12, 2023, pages 4-5. John was ordained deacon 19 December 1987.
60 See Bishop Jeff Driver's treatment of the Anglican church's response to the sexual abuse crisis in *Grey Spaces: Searching out the Church in the Shadows of Abuse*, (Eugene, OR: Wipf and Stock Publishers, 2022).
61 Tom Frame. *Church for a Nation: A History of the Anglican Diocese of Canberra and Goulburn*, (Alexandria, NSW: Hale and Ironmonger, 2000).

Barlow and Clements; he was not strategic as Warren or the later Browning, while Burgman was "in a class of his own". I thought Tom's insight was apt – "Owen wasn't captivated by process. It would assist, not restrain him".

Now there is a need to record a turn of events that led to Owen having to resign as a diocesan Bishop.

Chapter 10

Resignation from the diocese

It was 'front page news' in early 1992. Owen was charged for a minor offence: soliciting for sexual services in Bendigo. There were some embarrassing details. The incident involved an off-duty policeman when same sex-relationships were not as socially accepted. And some commented on the location: a public toilet. Certainly, it could be said Owen engaged in conduct unbecoming of a bishop, but I think it was sad that homosexual people were encouraged, if not forced, to contain and hide their sexuality. Eventually, reason prevailed and the charges were dropped by the Victorian Director of Public Prosecutions. He noted that the allegations were trivial and victimless. And it was not deemed to be in the public interest given the probable effect on Owen's health.

There was some sensational and intrusive press coverage especially by Mr Derryn Hinch. This was highly traumatising for the family. I think it is reasonable in a biography to draw some implications from this incident. While Owen married twice, it seems likely that his primary attraction was to same-sex partners. I heard from numerous people that Owen had been active in the gay scene for some time, and the encounter suggests that he had grown careless. At the time he was charged with the offence, he admitted the substance of the allegation to the police.

Owen did not go into any details in his interview with Graham Downie. He acknowledged, "I certainly had a very difficult year in 1992. I think I had been under a lot of pressure from a whole lot of directions really ... The shadows in our lives are necessary parts of our life. We have to embrace the darker side of our experience as well as the brighter, lighter side, whereas sometimes in religion it is almost as if that is denied and we are meant to be ever so happy, joyful; no depressive thoughts and the immediate remedy of faith as it were".

A member of Owen's support group commented that he was an enigma. While Owen was open and seemingly transparent, there was a side to his life he did not share. Perhaps it was hinted at, for example, he shared about a church organist in Victoria who would go to Sydney to have homosexual encounters, but felt guilty about the subterfuge. Later, this clergy person, after the Bendigo incident, speculated that Owen was talking about himself.

Then Archdeacon Jeff Driver was at the installation of the Rev'd Keith Groundwater into a rural parish, when Owen said to him, "Jeffrey, I am in trouble". This was the day that the news broke. The Rev'd Keith McCollim was in the car with Owen driving back to Canberra. Mary rang Owen and told him there were journalists and media outside the house. Keith's wife, the Rev'd Ann Dittmar-McCollim, was touched when Owen asked her permission to stay the night at their place. The next day, he went to the Rev'd Colin and Ms Dorothy Tunbridge's.[62] Keith became Owen's spiritual director until he and Gloria left Canberra.

After he was charged, Owen rang Peter Williams to tell him what had happened. Peter considered the incident to be an act of desperation – a person pushed to the edge emotionally by conservative sections of the church.

The incident happened in April 1992. The diocese did not have an assistant bishop since Ian George had gone to be the Archbishop of Adelaide. The diocesan archdeacon, the Ven. Allan Huggins, took on additional responsibilities including the role of chair of Bishop-in-council. A previous assistant Bishop in the diocese, the Rt Rev'd Neville Chynoweth, filled in with some Episcopal roles. Owen had intended to nominate an assistant bishop, but did not

---

62 Later Mary Gilmore cared for them in their deteriorating years, "I did it for dad."

consider it possible in the circumstances. Owen continued doing some of his normal diocesan tasks, but he also took time off. He had a significant amount of accumulated leave, which included some sick-leave. Owen sought places of refuge. He went to Bathurst and stayed with Bishop Bruce and Ms Zandra Wilson.

In the minutes of Bishop-in-Council, the incident was noted, 'events in recent days relating to the Bishop and alleged incidents which have been given wide media attention'.[63] The need to protect him from a legal point of view was noted and a motion was drafted to be read in parishes on the following Sunday. Motion 4613/92 included 'The Bishop-in-Council of the Diocese of Canberra and Goulburn met on Friday 10 April in Canberra. Members of Council express their unanimous and unqualified support, love and care for their Bishop and friend, Owen Dowling. Bishop Dowling is a man of great courage, integrity, wisdom and leadership. His work is greatly appreciated by all members of Council'.

Bishop Jeff Driver thought that the media were sympathetic to Owen. "They regarded him as one of the good guys." They recognised his progressive stance on women's ordination and other issues. There was also wide support from the community who are not so hung up on issues of sexual preference.

The clergy of the diocese had various opinions on what Owen should do. Should he resign? Should he step aside for a time? Should he continue? At least one of the rural deaneries did a straw poll with the result that a small majority favoured resignation. Bishop Owen was told of the vote, and it may have given some impetus to his resignation. There were some ugly incidents. One of the Evangelical clergy went to see Owen and using the example of King David being exposed by Nathan the prophet, told him a parable and dramatically announced "You are the man!" (2 Samuel 12:1-5). While some might see this harsh condemnation as understandable, no compassion or understanding was evident.

---

63 Page 240.

Sadly, the church has been described as an institution that 'shoots its wounded'.

It was a difficult time. I was serving as Rector of Holy Covenant, Jamieson. We asked Owen to come to a Sunday service and the parish presented him with a book of photographs and tributes to commemorate his ministry. A number of parishes did something similar. There was a farewell dinner at Mr Clive and Ms Lynlea Rodger's, attended by lay leaders in the diocese.

In the previous year, Bishop Owen had made the discussion of sexuality the major theme of his Synod address (2-4 August 1991). The Ven David Oliphant had assumed a part-time, but controversial role of chaplain to the sex industry in Canberra. Owen defended him in the strongest of terms – "a converted Christian excepts 100% responsibility for himself or herself and their decisions or lifestyle".[64] Owen saw a therapeutic role for sex workers, "though I can't speak with precise knowledge, it may be that some men who can act out their sexual fantasies with the sex worker who knows how to keep control are saved from doing such things and worse".[65] He concluded with the thought that the church must enter creatively and positively into this area with the spirit and the mind of Christ.

At the next Synod (31 July–2 August 1992), Owen declared his intention to retire 1 January 1993. He laid his staff on the altar of the cathedral on 20 December 1992 after 9 years as Bishop of Canberra and Goulburn.

In the minutes of Bishop-in-Council 12 June 1992, it was recorded, 'The Bishop advised that he had come to the decision, prior to his meeting with the archdeacons at 1 p.m. that day to seek an early retirement from his position as Bishop of the diocese'. He indicated that this would occur towards the end of the year and that he would take four months of leave that was due to him. This delay would allow him to attend General Synod in early July 1992 and give his vote for the ordination of women. The reason for this

---

64 Synod address, 1991, page 6-7.
65 1991, page 7.

decision was noted. Events 'had given rise to perceptions, some not based on fact, and had reached the point where his ministry, at least among some of the clergy and parishes, would be controversial. This reality led him to the conclusion that his state of health, as a result of the stress and strain on him as a result of controversy with the Metropolitan over the ordination of women and allegations made against him, was such that it would not be possible to regain an equilibrium and leave the diocese into a new period ministry'.[66] Additionally, 'He sought the support of Bishop-in-Council in being able to conclude his ministry with dignity and to minimise the talk and innuendo that had been hurtful and damaging to himself and his family'.[67]

The diocesan synod was held in Bega (31 July to 2 August 1992). It was during that synod that the official farewell was included as part of the program. The Archbishop of Sydney was present for the occasion. As Bishop Owen concluded his farewell speech, almost all the synod members rose to applaud his ministry in the diocese. However, the Archbishop of Sydney remained seated. I would also note the practical support of Bishop-in-Council to Owen at this time. The committee, in motion 4696/92, agreed to supplement his retirement package. Owen was 58 years old, and his superannuation was paid up to the age of 65, at an extra cost of $22,000. They also agreed, in motion 4697/92, to pay Owen $10,000 per annum for any interim period until he got a new stipendiary position, even if it was to age 65.

Owen's life continued in a new direction. In his words, "I started to have a deep friendship with Gloria Helen Goodwin who worked in the diocesan office. She was the manager of the development fund. We decided to get married, and it seemed to be wise to think about a move away from my job and to maybe do some parish work somewhere". However, there were some obstacles to the marriage. Gloria was a divorced person. In the Anglican Church, only the diocesan bishop could give permission

---

66 Page 256.
67 Page 257.

for divorcees to marry in the church. Owen resigned from the diocese, and they were eventually granted permission.

The marriage of Owen and Gloria was on the first day of his retirement. It was celebrated by the Reverend Keith McCollim. Keith took St Paul's letter to the Colossians as the starting point for his address. The Reverend Vicky Cullen, ordained to the priesthood by Bishop Dowling in the previous month, celebrated the Eucharist. She was the first woman to do so in St Paul's Church, Manuka. She said it was a privilege and joyous occasion. Owen said after the service, "We can spend a whole new life together; it's wonderful". Peter Williams thought that Gloria brought to Owen dimensions he needed. Owen was aware that some might think his marriage to Gloria was a convenience. Keith said, "Rubbish! They loved each other and their relationship began 12 to 18 months before".

Owen found a way to keep serving in the church. "I arranged to resign from the diocese and to seek some parish work elsewhere where I would be subject to a lot less pressure and, to some extent, be removed from the controversies that had surrounded me." After looking at possibilities overseas, they decided to remain in Australia. A friend, the Bishop of Tasmania, Phillip Newell, offered Owen a position in Hobart.

Sometimes good things come out of the darkest of events. Perhaps this can be seen in Owen's return to parish ministry, in which he always excelled, and in having time to contribute to the life of the wider church. But it was deeply disappointing that Owen could no longer serve as a diocesan bishop. There was much that he wanted to do in Canberra and Goulburn, but he had to step back and leave the diocese to his successor Bishop George Browning.

Chapter 11

On to Tasmania

For Owen, moving to Tasmania was an opportunity to discover more about his heritage. His great-great-grandfather was the Rev'd Henry Dowling, who came to Van Diemen's Land in 1834 as the first Baptist minister. A few years earlier, Owen's great-grandfather, John Dowling, had come out as a boy to work for a relative on Ellenthorpe in the midlands. This property eventually became a girls' school. Eventually, John Dowling ran a local farm called Verwood next to the school.

He persuaded others in his family to move to Tasmania. His older brother, Henry junior, came in 1832 to the Launceston area, eventually becoming the second mayor. He was also a publisher. Owen thought that he might have pirated copies of *The Pickwick Papers*. Henry was in the anti-transportation movement and was notable for introducing reticulated fresh water to the town. Henry was a good Baptist, like his father, and hoped to get 'sinners' off alcohol.

The Rev'd Henry Dowling senior came from pastoral ministry in Colchester, UK. It would appear that his motive for coming to the 'end of the earth', in Tasmania, was to evangelise convicts. Henry senior received a government grant to support this ministry to convicts who worked on the roads. He established the Baptist church in Launceston. Robert, the youngest, became a famous portrait artist. After the death of John in the 1860s, the Dowling family dispersed, mostly to the mainland. Owen had a painting of his ancestor Robert, a garden scene which had been handed down in the family. Later, Owen's relatives became Anglican through John marrying Cecilia who was a very devout Anglican.

Owen returned to parish ministry in Tasmania. He was convinced that it was a good move for a Bishop to do this prior to retirement, possibly following Bishop Warren's example in going to England. The parish of St James, New Town, was vacant and suitable. Bishop Philip Newell wanted Owen to be the Archdeacon of Hobart and to help him with the administration of the diocese. Owen was to serve in Tasmania for seven years prior to retiring to live in Canberra.

St James Church New Town

Some parishioners felt that Bishop Phillip had imposed Owen on the parish. But Owen soon felt at home. "The parish [of New Town] wanted me and they were very welcoming. Right from the beginning, the New Town people, and the people in the diocese generally, made us feel very much at home. I think that there is a certain separation in Tasmania from the life of the mainland. They take their own independent stance." Owen did not consider the parish appointment a 'come-down' for a bishop. All ministry is ministry, and equally important. He enjoyed going 'back to the ranks'. But he found synod challenging because he recognised what was being done poorly in the diocese and couldn't do anything about it.

Mr Peter Wise remembered Owen and Gloria being warmly accepted in the parish. Apparently, Owen held small charismatic services in St Andrews mid-week. He recalled an occasion on which Owen and others in the parish were interested in what was later called the Toronto Blessing. On one occasion, Owen was about to speak but felt paralysed. This was explained as, "Satan held me down". He needed help from other people to be able to go to the microphone. Later that night, when he went to his car, he found that all his tyres are been slashed! Owen interpreted these unusual events as spiritual warfare.

Owen also exercised what charismatic Christians would call the gift of prophecy. He was praying for people in the service and, over the previous three years, Peter's wife Vicki had been troubled by abdominal issues. Owen had no way of knowing about her health difficulties, but he was inspired to say to her, "The doctors will find the cause of your health issue shortly and fix it". This literally happened through a surgical procedure.[68]

Mr Geoff and Ms Muriel Cornish, of Lenah Valley Hobart, recalled the faithful pastoral ministry of Owen, especially in taking Holy Communion to Muriel's house-bound mother. He also had services of healing with the laying on of hands. Geoff remembered a series of five sermons that Owen gave on the topic of 'The Healing God'.

Owen challenged himself to continue playing both organ and piano. The organ at St James was being rebuilt. There was a great deal of effort in fundraising while work was done on the organ. When his son, Tim, visited from Holland they put on a recital. Tim was an accomplished trombone player. Bishop Phillip sang with them. The event drew a large crowd.

---

68 See http://www.about-i-am.net/oz_prophecy for a full account.

Owen was in New Town for 3½ years. He was asked to assume responsibility for the original church of St Johns which was built in the convict era and St James was added to the parish early in the 20th Century. Again, ministry was demanding. There were eight institutions, including various aged care facilities. A range of people were in care, including the blind and those with physical and mental disabilities. Owen was expected to offer chaplaincy. Gloria, an experienced lay chaplain, shared in the responsibility. Owen had the assistance of a curate.

Owen was in the New Town parish when a tragedy hit Tasmania: The Port Arthur massacre. Martin Bryant, who killed 35 and wounded 23 people, lived only a street away from the rectory.

Owen was one of six members of the Australian Heritage Commission. This commitment lasted for the first three years he was in Tasmania. He made a significant contribution to their work. He attended meetings in every capital city of Australia and a number of regional centres. The scope of the commission included natural heritage, built heritage and Aboriginal heritage. Owen worked closely with Professor Haig Beck on which buildings were to be placed on the national register. It was convenient that Owen lived in Tasmania because of the number of important heritage buildings on the island.

Owen acknowledged some depression after he moved to Tasmania. "I was the one that made the decision to resign, in the circumstances, and I made that decision I think after careful thought. But I didn't have anyone to really counsel me or persuade me otherwise. No one tried to persuade me the other way round. I suppose I often wondered whether I would have been better to have stayed."

There was a stark difference: a life not in the spotlight and less media pursuit. It was difficult for Owen to process what had happened. He kept a spiritual diary. He also wrote several poems to work though things emotionally. He continued, "When I look back now, I realise that a lot of my life hadn't been very reflective. It had been full charge ahead all the time and deep involvement, but you know, you got whisked from one thing to another. What I have learnt I think, in hindsight, is to be more reflective, to process things more, to take seriously the painful and hurtful things that happen to me and not just brush them off as I think I have perhaps been inclined to do before. I think that is a healthier thing".

Eventually, Owen was given something of an ultimatum from his GP, who said, "I think you ought to resign". Owen was diagnosed with age-onset diabetes. Previousl, he had heart bypass surgery and at times suffered from gout. Owen talked with his bishop about the availability of a less demanding rural parish. Owen was offered the parish of Longford-Perth, which included two towns in the north of Tasmania, just south of Launceston. Also in the parish, there were two small country churches – Bishopsbourne and Illawarra.

The parish of Longford had been established in 1830. There was a historic 1839 church, which was considered a fine example of colonial architecture. Owen and Gloria considered this an attractive place to live, being in the country and having ready access to Launceston (about a 20 minute drive away).

Christ Church Longford

Owen did not leave controversy behind him on the mainland. His friend Bishop Shelby Spong came to visit him in Tasmania on two occasions, speaking in both parishes. Spong was a prominent liberal in the Episcopal Church (that is the Anglican church in the USA) and his ministry was very controversial. Owen was elected area dean in both parishes in which he served in Tasmania.

At Eskleigh, in the Longford parish, there was fortnightly service for brain-damaged people. Both Owen and Gloria would attend. "We got to love this ministry with people who were imprisoned in bodies where they found it hard to express themselves. That was a beautiful ministry." There was Lesley who could not speak. She was severely spastic, but she could sing the words 'Praise God'. Owen taught the congregation to sing the words Praise God to the tune of *Amazing Grace*. Praise God would feature at communion services, much to the delight of the congregation.

Near Christ Church was a psychiatric unit which Owen called the 'Howard Hill Mob'. Some of these patients would come to church but predictably there would be difficulties. One of which Gloria resolved nicely. Margaret would insist on drinking the whole chalice of wine when she came forward. Apparently, she had an eating disorder. This led to the awful situation when the person administering the chalice would wrestle with her to try to recover the chalice. Wine would be spilt with general unhappiness being the result. Gloria asked Margaret to help her, she said, "Now, you know that at the end of the service Owen has to finish the chalice ... He drives off to another service and I don't really like him to have too much wine. So perhaps you could help by coming at the very end of the line and then you could finish the chalice". This worked very well.

Owen belonged to the Organ Historical Trust. He was pleased about the work being done in Australia to preserve historic pipe organs. This had been noticed overseas. Indeed, many of the standards developed here, relating to the Burra Charter, were being adopted in other countries.

Owen reflected on his emotional state in going to Tasmania. The transition was difficult. "When I first went to Hobart, I think I probably was more depressed than I realised ... If you go to a new job, a new home, a new marriage and a whole lot of new things that they are all high stressors really. I could agree with that in hindsight, though at the time I thought I was doing fine." He would go for walks and often thought about the convicts who were sent to Tasmania, but then he thought about the water that separated Tasmania from the mainland –from "The places that I was familiar with and where I wanted to be; the sort of feeling of being far off. That stayed with me. It helped me in a way, once I could put a name to it, a name to the feelings that I had. I felt a certain claustrophobia there I think, in Hobart and in Tasmania. I could not quite put words to it. I like it, visually speaking, and I like it, historically speaking, but I felt somehow or other caged or trapped. I suppose it was partly all the things that had happened to me and these sudden changes that had happened in my life."

He discussed this with Gloria and later with the Rev'd Eric Cave, a hospital chaplain, who became his spiritual companion. Owen arranged to speak to him once a month. "I think that as I talked with him and as I explained to him how I saw things, and as I could put words to it, I felt a lot better. I could understand what was happening to me."

Now Owen and Gloria faced another transition – retirement. After many decades in demanding ministries, Owen had accomplished more than most clergy would consider possible. But leaving Tasmania was an end that began to look like another beginning.

Chapter 12

Retirement

Owen was ready to lay down his professional responsibilities. He wanted the luxury of time to follow the priorities he set. He reflected, "In some ways, I see it more clearly now, how the various threads of my life have come together towards the end of my ministry and now going into my retirement. Especially how my own experience in music, liturgy and worship, and then the ministry in general, was able to be put to use in the preparation of the hymnbook. The fact that I am really now in a position to speak very knowledgeably about the background to the hymnbook".

Owen and Gloria decided to return to Canberra. They considered various options, but Canberra had some advantages. Gloria's father was still alive, and she had a daughter and son living in Canberra. Gloria owned a house in Red Hill which had been leased while they were in Tasmania. Both Owen and Gloria enjoyed spending time with their grandchildren. Owen was a much loved grandpa!

Once back, Owen and Gloria did a courtesy call on the diocesan Bishop George and Ms Browning. While he did not refer to this in his interview with the journalist, Owen said to me that he was hurt by what he felt was a cool reception. In fairness to Bishop George, he found Owen's participation in diocesan events something of a challenge and unexpected of a retired bishop in his former diocese, but he tolerated it without comment.

When Owen returned to Canberra from Tasmania, he worshipped at St Paul's, Manuka. Initially, the Rector was Archdeacon Jeff Driver who believed that Owen had made significant progress in integrating his experiences since retiring as a diocesan. "Sex is messy. There was an authenticity and honesty about him, he had made a deep journey, working through his issues and experiences." There was no denial or attempt to mask what happened. Owen was trying to bring together his different experiences which Jeff saw as a "God sign".

The rector who followed Jeff was the Rev'd Dr Scott Cowdell. He encouraged Owen to assume a pastoral and episcopal role in the parish. He was, for example, invited to bless the newly acquired bells. He also preached and celebrated the eucharist on a regular basis. However, Scott received some negative responses. He received two vicious anonymous (typed!) letters that were highly critical of having Owen do any public ministry. This appears to have been a continuation of the previous poison pen letters.

Tom Frame welcomed Owen to contribute to the life of St Mark's National Theological Centre. Tom was the first former student to become its director. He recognised Owen's expertise in liturgy, church music and pastoral care. Owen was appointed a liturgical and musical consultant and contributed to the Diploma of Anglican Orders program over the next four years. This was a role that helped him shape the emerging generation of clergy in the diocese. He would assist ordinands to prepare weekly services of worship and offered insightful feedback. It was obvious that the students developed an easy rapport with Owen and gained an understanding of the challenges of episcopal leadership and the need to consider closely the varied contexts in which public services were conducted.

Over the years, Owen had shown a broad and inclusive approach to worship. He appreciated contemporary music,. "Well, you can have it very well done. I mean the Geoff Bullock style music with Hillsong and so on, that has come out of the Pentecostal churches in Sydney. They are great, but actually they take some skill to perform and perform well." He noted that such music has a personal focus in being renewed and refreshed in the Spirit. The corporate dimension of worship can be somewhat neglected.

Owen also appreciated contemporary trends in hymns that express themes such as social justice and caring for the environment.

Owen maintained his musical skills in retirement. This included singing with the Canberra Choral Society. He played the organ for the occasional wedding, funeral and church service. When he travelled overseas, he always took music with him and opportunities opened up. He visited Tim in Holland. They would both travel to various churches to try out historic organs *in situ*. Owen also travelled to various parts of Australia to give seminars on the hymnbook.

The healing ministry with the Order of St Luke was another post-retirement commitment. He gave seminars in various places. In his words, "I was the Australian warden for six years and then I became state chaplain in Tasmania. In recent times I have taken up the position again. We have re-established the chapter of the Order of St Luke only several weeks ago here in Canberra and I have become the chaplain again. I have been asked to be the regional south-east and western region, south-western region of New South Wales, to be the regional chaplain."

Owen sought to present a theologically sound and balanced approach to the healing ministry. One that was responsive to the needs of the individual seeking healing. Sensibly he observed, "Forgiveness and living in peace with another person or with yourself may be more important than even having a physical healing. But on the other hand, I also realise that physical healings do take place and one of the good things about it is that we never really know whether it was the prayer or the medicine or the advice the doctor gave or whatever. It is a whole combination of things".

Owen wrote two small books on healing. The first was *Channels of Healing: Studies for the People of God*, (Wantirna, Victoria: Order of St Luke the Physician, 2002) with 30 study chapters. At the end of this book is an address 'Caution, Boldness, Presumption: Our Need for a Discerning Spirit'.[69] This was

---

69 Pages 63-70.

followed by *Searching Questions on Healing: A Christian Perspective*, (Wantirna, Victoria: Order of St Luke the Physician, 2005) with 20 study chapters.[70]

Owen was sought out for 'spiritual direction'. He drew on his broad experience in ministry and people sought his wise counsel.

Clearly Owen enjoyed being retired. "Yes, I just love it. I can do the things that I am interested in doing. I have got enough things to do to keep me interested and occupied. Yet, on the other hand, I do not have to do things. I can say no. I can say yes or no, so I can spread them out a bit, and I have been doing that a little bit and making sure I don't get too hectic." This included reading, writing personal letters and attending lectures. He added, "I really do enjoy it and get a lot of pleasure from my life and from my marriage with Gloria and the things that we are able to do together. We trip around together and she helps me with the seminars, and we can talk about them afterwards, that is all to the good." Interestingly, Owen did not embrace the internet. He would go to a local library to receive and send emails but he did not have a computer at home.

In his life, Owen achieved a sense of integration. For him, retirement made "good use of the experience that I have had in life. It is like the threads of my life coming and each now finding its significant place. I thought that I would be doing locums and I don't and in many ways, I am pleased not to be doing that ... You know, you go back and you are suddenly immersed in running a parish again. Whereas, I am able to use my particular gifts, my specialist gifts, you could say, to good effect. That seems to me to be a good solution."

---

[70] ISBN 978-0-908460-30-4. Interestingly, Study 13 "Is it a valid ministry to cast out spirits? How is it done?" (pp. 52-56). He acknowledged the reality of evil spirits, but included significant cautions. He cautioned about doing exorcisms and "moving into what could be called presumption and putting ourself in the place of God ... we remain fallible creatures of God, who make mistakes and fail to listen to God, blinded perhaps by our determination to win through and prove we have been on the right track. There is a time for stepping back and admitting we are in deeper water than we know." *Channels of Healing*.

He had an unfulfilled ambition. "There is one other thing that I did promise myself, that I would write, do some writing. This series [of recorded interviews] might prompt me to get ahead and write what I had thought to do, which are some cameos of my life, my interest in life and to actually get that down in a form that either could be preserved or published." I hear in these words Owen's approval of my attempt to capture aspects of his life, especially as I am drawing so heavily on what he recalled as significant.

Owen looked towards the future with some optimism. He believed that good hymnody and good psalmody would last. He could see that the core of the Christian faith would still have an international expression, but he hoped that it would not be too fundamentalist in style. Maybe Christians would be humble enough to learn from one another. He welcomed a spirit of freedom, in what was believed and how faith was expressed. He had an inter-faith perspective and hoped that religion could prove to be a positive force in the world, though he acknowledged that this had not always been the case.

He cited the example of Jesus. "Surely Jesus came to help to restore that and to give people a sense of perspective and not get all caught up in being so fussy about all the details. But I am very much more down the inclusive rather than the exclusive way of approaching religious faith. I believe in the spirit of Jesus that we should include and affirm one another rather than get terribly exclusive ... To be firm about the basic kind of essentials that we wish to proclaim, but not in a way that rubbishes others or excludes others. This will be a great challenge to us, I think, to be able to do that. To have a kind of stability about who we are and what we are, and yet at the same time an openness and flexibility."

Gill Varcoe recalled that, in the period before his death, Owen asked to see the women priests that he had ordained at the end of 1992. A number did see him, but Gill did not. She was uncertain why. Perhaps "unease" was a good word and, "I had nothing to say to him".

The Rev'd Dr Ross Kingham, a Uniting Church minister, knew Owen well. He described Owen in his last year, facing certain death, but being 'utterly undaunted'. When Ross was in hospital following prostate surgery, he encountered Owen on the next ward and shared a painful experience. The previous night in bed, Ross's foot became entangled with his catheter tube and it had 'popped out!' Owen recounted an incident when his mother was in dementia care, she visited a man with a catheter. When she left, she thought the tube was the handle of her handbag – with a predictable result!

Matthew, his son, recalled that his father was losing his voice because of throat cancer. In a whisper, he summoned his family around the piano and they sang the hymns he wanted at his funeral service. One of them was a hymn which he had written himself that contained the word 'inclusivity'. Although very well-intentioned, it is a five-syllable word which did not lend itself to poetry. Nor did it sit comfortably with the metre. They all fell about laughing as they tried to sing the word to the music. Matthew added, "Even with tears in our eyes, we were able to laugh with him".

Owen died on 7 May 2008. He was 73 years old. The funeral was held at St Paul's, Manuka on May 16. It was a parish he had once been offered. The service was a clear tribute to how many lives Owen had touched in his ministry and life. After his death, Gloria became a novice in the Community of the Holy Name. She died in 2020.[71]

Reflection

Jesus called imperfect people to follow him. This included a couple of fishermen, a tax collector, a zealot and a traitor. There were also women, including a wealthy aristocrat and Mary Magdalene – a sex worker according to church tradition A mixed bunch who accomplished great things. Any theology of ministry must begin with imperfect people, who nevertheless are called by God and sometimes do what can justly be termed miraculous. Few illustrate this fundamental truth better than Owen Dowling. He achieved remarkable things in diverse areas of ministry.

I think it is also worth reflecting on the obstacles Owen overcame to achieve all this. He was sexually abused as a child. He supported Beverly through highly personal attacks, periods of severe depression and self-medication with alcohol. I think it is likely that Owen struggled with same sex attraction, in a time of less social acceptance, and at least for a time after losing Beverly he had a second life. This private side of his life was exposed on the front page of national media. He resigned his diocese and yet, undaunted, he continued to serve in ministry. He 'finished the course' (2 Timothy 4:7). God can ask no more of those who serve him.

I think Owen can inspire all who serve in ministry. We fall short of our ideals and most certainly the 'glory of God' (Romans 3:23). But we experience grace. Thankfully. And do what we can to make a difference.

Appendix 1
Publications

Music and an Australian Prayer Book. AIO Press. 1978. ISBN 978-0-908089-15-4. with Lawrence Bartlett

Searching Questions on Healing: A Christian Perspective. Order of Saint Luke The Physician in Australia. 2005. ISBN 978-0-908460-30-4. with Steven Hallam

Power to Be Witnesses. Anglican Information Office. 1988. ISBN 978-0-949108-81-4.

Plaque at St Saviour's Cathedral, Goulburn

Appendix 2
Other contributors

The Reverend Canon Professor Scott Cowdell, theologian, Diocese Canberra and Goulburn.

The Rev'd Dr Ross Kingham UCA minister, previously Director, Barnabas Ministries, Inc.

Dr Janet Scarfe, national president, Movement for the Ordination of Women 1989-95

The Rev'd Andrew Knight previously senior military chaplain (Group Captain, RAAF)

The Rev'd Allan Huggins previously Dean of Sale and Diocesan Archdeacon, Canberra and Goulburn (1989-1999)

Dr Graeme Yapp lay-reader, retreat leader with Eremos and prominent layman.

The Rev'd Canon Kevin Stone parish priest in the diocese of C&G.

The Rev'd Robin Miners who served as a priest in the diocese for 38 years.

The Rev'd David Clark parish priest in the diocese of C&G.

The Very Rev'd Peter G. Williams, AM, RC priest and Vicar General Diocese of Paramatta

Mr Bob Arthur prominent lay leader in diocese of C&G

Mr Clive and Lynlea Rodger prominent lay leaders in the diocese

Appendix 2 Other contributors

The Rev'd Dr Chris Simon parish priest and academic.

The Rev'd Anne Dudzinski parish priest in the diocese.

Sheila Thompson (organist at St John's Reid 35 years).

The Rev'd Elaine Gifford parish priest in the diocese.

The Rev'd Canon Gill Varcoe Served in diocese 1987-2020.

The Venerable Desmond McGuire Emeritus Archdeacon C&G.

The Rt Rev'd Dr George V. Browning, Bishop of Canberra and Goulburn (1993-2008).

Tom Frame, former Bishop to the Australian Defence Force (2001-2007) and later a research professor at UNSW Canberra (2014-2023).

The Rev'd Keith McCollim served as hospital chaplain and CPE supervisor.

The Rev'd Canon Ann Dittmar-McCollim served in parish ministry and chaplaincy.

Mr Peter Wise Layperson in New Town parish, Hobart.

Mr Geoff and Mrs Muriel Cornish, he as Lay-reader and she as sacristan in New Town, Hobart.

The Rt Rev'd Dr Jeff Driver, who served in Canberra and Goulburn, then later as Bishop of Gippsland and Archbishop of Adelaide (2005-2016).

Rev'd Tassie Pappas who served in the Diocese of Melbourne and Diocese of Wangaratta.

www.ingramcontent.com/pod-product-compliance
Lightning Source LLC
Chambersburg PA
CBHW011953090526
44591CB00020B/2748